SELLSATION!

Praise for *SELLsation!*

"*A witty, informative A to Z primer for reaching and impacting on that all-important market of women professionals, executives and entrepreneurs.*"
~Chris Madden, TV host, and founder and CEO of Chris Madden, Inc., a multimedia company encompassing publishing, design, licensing and television

"*Leslie's knowledge, insight and experience, distilled in her wonderful book, will help any company develop their strategy and expand their reach into this lucrative market. Putting her strategies into practice, including our sponsorship of Women's Leadership Exchange, has helped BellSouth position ourselves to the female residential consumer, small business owner and executive as the telecommunications provider of choice.*"
~Janet McKinley, BellSouth Chief Corporate Auditor, and founder and president of the BellSouth Women's Networking Alliance

"*I could not put SELLsation! down. As well as a critical roadmap, it is such fun to read! Companies that adhere to Leslie Grossman's 7-Step C.R.E.A.T.E.S. program will most certainly enhance their company's profitability and at the same time receive accolades from the women's business and networking community at large.*"
~Judy George, founder and CEO of Domain Home Fashions, Inc. and co-author of *The Intuitive Businesswoman*

"*As the owner of three minority and women owned businesses, I found Leslie Grossman's book SELLsation! valuable, credible and accurate as it is filled with ready to activate and implement bottom line strategies all business professionals need to know. She does not waste valuable time with fluffy, ego stroking flowery language, but cuts to the chase with advice that is based on practical application and field experience, and then backed up with market research, impressive data and successful market penetration. This book is a must have for any professional wanting to expand sales to women business owners...without wasting any time! Kudos, Leslie! Another success on a rather extensive list. Your commitment to your passion is evident.*"
~Valerie Red-Horse, founder and owner of Red-Horse Native Productions, the Red-Horse Securities Investment Bank and Red-Horse Financial Group

"*Leslie Grossman is the best in this arena, and SELLsation! is clearly based on her decades of experience and the breakthrough success of Women's Leadership Exchange, which she and Andrea March designed to help women in business grow past plateaus. In this book she covers many, if not all, of the most intricate aspects of capturing the hearts, minds, and business of women entrepreneurs, executives and professionals.*"
~Linda Kaplan Thaler, CEO of The Kaplan Thaler Group and co-author of *Bang! Getting Your Message Heard In a Noisy World*

"I've known and worked with Leslie Grossman for over 20 years. Believe me when I say that she knows everything about the executive and entrepreneurial women's market. Take advantage of her generosity in sharing all that wisdom, and you too can capture the most exciting customer base of the decade."
~Edie Weiner, president of Weiner, Edrich, Brown, a leading futurist consulting group, and bestselling co-author of *FutureThink*

"In this book, Leslie Grossman provides a detailed road map to guide you to success in doing business with women business owners and leaders. Case studies and examples from her vast experience with corporations and women leaders bring her advice to life and identify best practices which you can put into use immediately."
~Sharon Hadary, Executive Director, Center for Women's Business Research

"If you're a busy professional who wants a comprehensive guide to engaging this huge and growing market, this will surely be the most important book you'll ever read. Leslie's seven steps and real-life examples take you on a 360-degree tour of what you should do—and who you should know—to successfully engage this marketplace."
~Gail Evans, bestselling author of *Play Like a Man, Win Like a Woman: What Men Know About Success that Women Need to Learn*

"The C.R.E.A.T.E.S. 7-step program provides proven strategies based on Leslie's extensive business experience that will consistently generate success for women entrepreneurs, executives and professionals."
~Bruce Perkins, Vice President, Manager of Supplier Diversity and Business Development at Merrill Lynch and member of several WLE Advisory Boards

"Read and Reap! I have learned more from Leslie Grossman's on how to market to women business owners and other entrepreneurs than in any other book that purports to be about marketing to women. This is the bottom line truth about what really works today and as such is a must-read for every company."
~Rieva Lesonsky, editorial director, *Entrepreneur* and Entrepreneur Media, Inc. and co-author of *Start Your Own Business* and other books

"Leslie Grossman provides a set of smart business strategies that will yield tangible, measurable benefits for a company that puts them in play. Read, learn, apply, triumph with this red-hot market segment that will only continue to grow."
~Cary J. Broussard, former Senior Vice President of Wyndham Hotels, creator of WOMEN ON THEIR WAY® program, and author of *From Cinderella to CEO*

SELLSATION!

How Companies Can Capture Today's Hottest Market: Women Business Owners and Executives

LESLIE GROSSMAN

WPE Press LLC
14 Wall Street – 20th floor
New York NY 10005
212-618-1811
Toll free: 888-937-5800
www.sellsationbook.com

An application to register this book for cataloguing has been submitted to the Library of Congress.

ISBN 0-9772666-0-5

Book design by Bruce Jacobson

This book is dedicated to all the vibrant, determined, hardworking women I meet every day—business owners, leaders, executives, professionals—and the companies that show they care by supporting the growth of our businesses.

It's a perfect match, and I am proud to be the matchmaker

CONTENTS

Acknowledgements

How does one acknowledge a lifetime of a loving family, personal friends, business associates, business friends, clients, sponsors, gurus, leaders, speakers and role models that have inspired and supported me in becoming the person I am today?

I often say I am the luckiest person in the world to have a family I adore, a business that inspires me each day, and the opportunity to meet thousands of incredible women and men who lead interesting, exciting and purposeful lives. I thank each and every person that I have met in the course of my many businesses, for they are why I created both B2Women and Women's Leadership Exchange, and they are why I wrote this book.

I particularly want to send huge hugs of appreciation to my parents, "creative" Charlotte and "optimistic" Jack, who are in my heart each day, and who set me on the track to become a caring, dedicated and committed human being. And to my husband and best friend of 30 years, Richie Abrams, who has always been my greatest cheerleader, telling me "You can do it" every time my confidence was shaken, and most importantly, for being a loving husband and wonderful co-parent, sharing responsibility in raising our two brilliant and loving children, Josh and Sara, two young adults well on their way to making their marks on the world. Thanks to my sister Beth, who always keeps me straight with her spiritual wisdom, and my brother Howard, who set me on the path of personal discovery and insight. Also affectionate thanks to my dear and patient friend Barbara Carlsen, an outstanding musician and educator, she helps me keep my head straight when my ego goes wandering.

Professionally, thanks to the National Association of Women

Business Owners (NAWBO), where I first discovered the magic of women supporting each other to build their businesses. That's where I met many of my mentors, including Sharon Emek, Whitney Johns Martin and Barbara Stanbridge, women who were willing to share their own experience to help me and other businesswomen address their greatest challenges. My other mentors, Sue Sussman, Marcia Cantarella, Vivian Shimoyamo, Diane Valletta and Sophia Corona, are women I lean on to help me see the clear picture when things get a bit cloudy. I have several "sisters" that I would walk on water for: Edie Weiner (yes, the Futurist), Ann Stock (formerly head of the White House Social Office and now the Kennedy Center) and Cary Jehl Broussard (who proved the women's business market was a huge payoff to companies). Not only are they brilliant and generous, but also they are the most fun people anyone could ever be with!

Thanks to Tony Smith of VSA Consulting, definitely the best business coach in the world. Not only did my business revenues of my previous firm, CMA, double while working with him, but I was also able to identify my bold stand "to create more women leaders in the world," which laid the groundwork for my future businesses—B2Women and Women's Leadership Exchange. In addition, I was fortunate to be a guinea pig in Gail Blanke's pilot *Lifedesigns* program, which gave me the power to visualize how to take my stand and create the life I wanted. Thanks to Janet Page of Bank of America, who gave me my first business loan when she was at Flushing Savings Bank, after having been turned down by five banks even though I had been in business ten years and was profitable.

Thank you to Richard D'Ambrosio of American Express. It was the assignment that Richard handed me, to identify sponsorship opportunities for a women business owner marketing initiative back in 1999, which caused me to see a huge void for women leading established companies. To this day, Richard continues to be a source of friendship and support. And to the foresight of Kerry Hatch, then General Manager of OPEN from American Express, who said "yes" to OPEN becoming presenting sponsor to an unproven program and thus launched Women's Leadership Exchange in 2002. It was Sue Tompkins of Northwestern Mutual who, as a client of B2Women, gave me the opportunity to take the C.R.E.A.T.E.S. strategy on the road to more than ten cities, and together we had a great time sharing it with the agents who were eager to capture this market. Thanks to Sharon Hadary, executive director of the Center for Women's Business Research, without whose statistics and research there would never be an understanding of the power of the women business owner market, and therefore, no need for the C.R.E.A.T.E.S. strategy, B2Women or Women's Leadership Exchange.

One of my biggest acknowledgements is to my business partner, Andrea March, who has also become my dear friend. Though she barely knew me, she saw the power of the C.R.E.A.T.E.S. strategy and the concept for Women's Leadership Exchange. She put her own business on hold in order to partner with me to create a revolutionary concept. Our partnership enabled me not only to further develop C.R.E.A.T.E.S., but also to put it into action at Women's Leadership Exchange.

Of course, none of my dreams would have been realized without the support of the incredible people behind the corporations that continue to support the continuing growth and expansion of Women's Leadership Exchange: Susan Sobbott, Lexi Brownell Reese, Catherine Foucher, Rita McCaffrey, Tom Sclafani and Channing Barringer of OPEN from American Express; Laura Hoffman and Marnie Omanoff, formerly of OPEN from American Express; Marilyn Johnson and Patti Ross of IBM; Caroline Gundeck, Bruce Perkins and Suba Barry of

Merrill Lynch; Cindy Bates and Aaron Bernstein of Microsoft; Lynn Connelly of Office Depot, Rieva Lesonsky of *Entrepreneur* Magazine; Pernille Spiers-Lopez and Astrid Oyo of IKEA; Andrea Somtz of *Forbes Magazine* and Janet McKinley of BellSouth. They are not only acting to benefit their companies, but are also committed to helping women in business realize their potential. These companies warrant our business.

A big part of the task of making this book happen was Judy Katz, who also serves the WLE as PR consultant. Judy helped me think through how to put my strategy into a book that could almost become a "textbook" to help companies reach this powerful market, and also be engaging and lively. Judy, with the able assistance of journalist Sharon McDonnell, a regular contributor to *The New York Times*, was my partner in this project.

And last, but far from least, thank you to the WLE team, who help me and Andrea put the C.R.E.A.T.E.S. strategy into action every day: Beckie Jankiewicz, Jami Kelmenson, Navin Gopwani, Jolene Zupnik, Lisa Kraus, Sue Erdreich and Jocelyn Fenyn.

I am grateful to all of you for the part you've played in changing the world.

Introduction

Why Tapping into 'The New Women's Network' Creates Loyal, Enthusiastic Customers Who Also Spread the Word About You!

by Andrea March

> *"We don't accomplish anything in this world alone...and whatever happens is the result of the whole tapestry of one's life and all the weavings of individual threads from one to another that creates something."*
>
> ~Sandra Day O'Connor (1930-)
> U.S. Supreme Court Justice

Women business owners and female executives today are reinventing mentoring and networking. Leslie and I describe this powerful process as "The New Women's Network." It is not new—*for men*. For women, it is nothing short of revolutionary. Men have always been part of extensive social networks, fraternities, clubs and associations. Men through the ages have always been willing to "help a buddy out." They network naturally and unselfconsciously at sporting events, on the golf course, at the water cooler and in the boardrooms. Well, women are beginning to do the same. Recognizing this, Leslie and I deliberately decided to move the process along.

We are now doing so for two synergistic groups. First, we are accelerating the process for all those dynamic, ambitious, hardworking women entrepreneurs who want to grow their businesses beyond their wildest dreams, and are, in fact, willing to help make this happen for other women business owners and for themselves. Secondly, we are making this work for companies smart enough to recognize a marvelous opportunity: the chance to engage with today's woman business owner, executive or professional in a meaningful way so that she will gladly become their devoted customer.

Many companies, of course—and yours may be one—do not know how to secure the goodwill (and continuing business) of customers or clients so that they come back to you again and again, even if the competition offers them something appealing. In addition to your customer's continuing business, this kind of brand loyalty means that your customers are expanding your reputation and further increasing your customer base and profitability.

In our fast-paced business world, the question is not whether or not we want customer enthusiasm and fidelity but *how* to gain it. How *does* a company accomplish the daunting task of putting together the WHY and HOW of marketing to businesswomen— and along the way, to all customers, men included?

That is precisely what this book is about. In these pages you will discover WHY you need to go out to women business owners and executives, listen carefully to them, and learn what this audience really wants from you. At the same time, you will learn HOW to give your customers what they want.

Leslie and I believe that the answer to rising above your competition to reach today's powerful market lies in her unique 7-Step C.R.E.A.T.E.S. strategy. This seven-step program, taken as a whole, will allow your company, no matter how large or small, to engage vigorously with women business owners.

I want to emphasize again that these seven strategies work equally as well for small or mid-size firms as they do for giant multinational companies.

Current research shows that women business owners are the fastest-growing, most lucrative, *hottest* new market segment to come along in decades—and they are only growing stronger, in numbers and in gross revenues. According to the Center for Women's Business Research, they represent a whopping 50% of all privately held businesses! This market is not one you can afford to miss out on. If *you* do not properly engage them, your competition will.

Ideally, you are already onboard with the critical importance of this kind of outreach—the WHY. The HOW part of the formula we offer you lies in the very nature of the multiple-channel, multimedia educational company Leslie and I formed in 2002, Women's Leadership Exchange (WLE), which operates under the guidelines of Leslie's 7-Step C.R.E.A.T.E.S. program.

WLE holds five conferences each year in five cities—New York, Atlanta, Southern California, Dallas and Chicago. At these events, companies that sponsor the conferences can interact directly with the 600 to 1,000 individual women entrepreneurs, executives and professionals who attend the full-day events. These women lead established companies that are positioned for major growth. Throughout the day, our attendees (whom we call "Keyholders") gain access to the tools and connections that propel their businesses. They gain this access through a) seminars and interactive learning sessions led by our "Growth Gurus," b) through keynote speeches by world-renowned women leaders from all walks of life, and c) through natural,

comfortable access to each other that is made possible by facili-
tated networking throughout the day.

Likewise, our sponsors benefit from WLE conferences because
our format positions them squarely on the playing fields with
these women. These sponsor/attendee connections take place at
roundtable discussions over breakfast and lunch, at the seminars, and at sponsor booths in the Interactive Information
Center. The schedule is set up in such a way that attendees visit
the Interactive Information Center in three distinct time peri-
ods. Additionally, sponsors are able to meet and get to know
attendees during several spontaneous opportunities for conver-
sation and engagement.

How a Momentous Collaboration Began
Leslie and I had individually each reached a critical point in our
entrepreneurial lives by the time we met in 2001. At that fortu-
itous meeting, we quickly discovered that we were in complete
agreement as to what resources were lacking for women business owners, specifically those who had gotten to a midpoint in
their growth and needed a boost from role models. We believed
that those role models would ideally be successful women entrepreneurs who could inspire and educate them, be available to
support their growth beyond what are often self-imposed
plateaus, and give them or show them how to find and use the
tools necessary to move ahead.

Leslie and I designed Women's Leadership Exchange as the
place where women could access all of these missing ingredients, and where the 7-Step C.R.E.A.T.E.S. program could be put
into play for corporations who offered the very products and
services these businesswomen want and need.

Leslie knew, from her own businesses and from active, leadership participation in major women's organizations, what these entrepreneurs and executives lacked in terms of financial and other skill sets, as well as what other types of support and connections would help foster their growth. Since she and I agreed so profoundly on what was needed, we decided to join forces. The result was Women's Leadership Exchange, and the brand-extending Women's Travel Exchange,[SM] which holds twice-yearly Women's Business Spa Retreats.

The WLE conferences are our bedrock. We also offer our Keyholders (so named because after one conference they hold the "key" to growth) a national online "New Women's Network Directory," and a free e-newsletter, "The Exchange." Our Women's Business Spa Retreats, which we hold under the name Women's Travel Exchange (WTE), also fill a need and are always sold out. At these luxurious, relaxing four-day "time-outs," women business owners have a rare opportunity to get to know each other and our sponsors in the most ideal networking atmosphere possible: golden sun and golden sands at a Golden Door or other four-star spa! By the way, we have also just initiated yet another extension of our brand—Women's Publishing Exchange[SM] (WPE). WPE will publish this book, and then reach out to other businesswomen who might want to have us help them actualize a book of their own.

Why This Partnership Works

Both Leslie and I are "serial entrepreneurs." I had run my jewelry import and distribution company, Andrea March Accessories, for 15 years. In 1997, I founded another company, Investment Expo, which I am proud to say quickly became the largest financial strategies trade show and seminar program in the Northeast and South Florida. Designed for the investing public, the event featured world-renowned investment experts and bestselling authors as speakers and seminar leaders. I had also signed on such corporate sponsors as *The New York Times,* CNBC, CNN and Fidelity Investments, to name a few. I had been running Investment Expo for four years when I met Leslie. The skills I brought to our collaboration were these: I knew how to run large, complicated special events for the public, and I knew how to engage national sponsors so that their ROI was substantive.

At the same time, there were whole areas where I was not as knowledgeable as I wanted to be. As it happens, those were the very areas in which Leslie excelled! So, seemingly by accident—although I, for one, do not believe in accidents—two women's lives collided and led us to form what has become an exciting and successful new entity.

At the time we met, Leslie was running B2Women, a company she founded in 2000 to support the growth objectives of her brand-name client companies. B2Women—which Leslie still heads—conceives and implements groundbreaking marketing and public relations initiatives for corporations, for women's business organizations, for conferences and for leading women-owned firms. As we do with Women's Leadership Exchange, Leslie's consulting arm, B2Women, helps companies connect to the fast-growing market segment of women business owners and business executives.

A New Way to Market to Women Business Owners
What Leslie and I both strongly believed, and still do, is that most corporate sponsorships are static, and generally fail to provide adequate return on sponsorship investment dollars. There's an old saying in advertising, "Let's run it up the flagpole and see what sticks." That kind of one-size-fits-all approach is a recipe for disaster. Today the customer is king, or better said, queen! You need a strategy *and* a place to implement it. What's

a great show without a theatre where people can see it? That's what WLE conferences are, a great place to take your show to your audience. Strategies and plans are great, but they need to be focused and realistic—and also need to "take place" somewhere, not just as a general ad campaign. It still surprises me to see how much money companies waste on generic advertising and marketing campaigns, which women, especially women business owners, rarely notice.

Leslie's clients and WLE sponsors have tested C.R.E.A.T.E.S. on the playing fields of life. In the pages that follow, you will read about their experiences with this step-by-step strategy, and see why WLE conferences are perfect examples of a venue where sponsors can jumpstart new campaigns with their specific target audiences and put them into play. An added benefit of this kind of "in the trenches" marketing is that, while infinitely more effective than standard generic, saturation advertising, it also costs far less than the high six or seven figures that ad campaigns can run.

Right from the launch of WLE, we were most fortunate in garnering thousands of conference attendees, connecting with even greater numbers of women business owners and executives via our Web site, and along the way engaging many national sponsors while also attracting a great deal of media attention. As a result of this immediate success, we realized we had filled a giant void, one that had previously been hidden in plain sight. We were, in fact, doing nothing less than changing the way companies market to women in business, owners, business executives and women professionals in solo or group practice. We also realized, to our mutual joy, that marketing this way was entertaining and educational. For us, having fun is a big part of the C.RE.A.T.E.S. program, WLE and everything we do!

I am delighted to report that our strategy likewise works for *us*. Because WLE conferences are built on the C.R.E.A.T.E.S. methodology, we have attracted enthusiastic brand-name companies that report they love the customized sponsorship programs we set up for them.

I think Leslie has done a great job with this book, and hope you enjoy it, and learn from it. And, if there is any way we can help you with your outreach to this critical new market, please, come talk to us.

And now...enjoy the journey!

Andrea March
Women's Leadership Exchange®
New York City, September, 2005

Chapter 1

The C.R.E.A.T.E.S·
7-Step Formula for
Marketing Successfully to Women
Business Owners, Executives and Professionals

> *They talk about a 'woman's sphere'*
> *As though it has a limit;*
> *There's not a spot on sea or shore,*
> *In sanctum, office, shop or store,*
> *Without a woman in it.*
>
> ~Author unknown
> (found in a 1905 book *Sovereign Woman Versus*
> *Mere Man* by Jennie Day Haines)

Let's hit the deck running, and face facts...There are many misconceptions about women in business. *You* may be exceptionally well-informed and need no convincing, but misinformation abounds about the power, scope and influence of this market sector, which is far more extensive and important than most business leaders and executives realize. Overlooking this market can, in both the short and long run, be dangerous to a company's bottom line, competitive edge and longevity.

Below are just a few of the more common misconceptions, along with the accurate information. Go down this short list and see if any of this information comes as a surprise.

Belief #1: The number of women-owned firms is growing just as fast as other firms in the United States.
*Fact: From 1997-2004 the number of women-owned firms with employees grew **twice as fast** as all U.S. firms with employees (17% vs. 9%).*

Belief #2: Women now own one-quarter of the businesses in the U.S.
*Fact: Nearly **half** (48%) of all privately owned U.S. businesses are now at least 50% owned by women.*

Belief #3: Women make half the consumer purchasing decisions in U.S. homes.
Fact: Women make 85% of all consumer purchasing decisions in U.S. homes.

Belief #4: Women-owned firms with over $1 million in revenues grew just as fast as other U.S. firms of that size.
*Fact: Women-owned firms with over $1 million in revenues grew nearly **twice** as fast (32%) as similarly sized firms in the U.S. from 1997-2000.*

Belief #5: One in 14 U.S. workers is employed by a woman-owned business!
*Fact: **One in 7** U.S. workers is employed by a woman-owned business!*

Belief #6: Men outnumber women in higher paying managerial and professional occupations by about 2:1.
*Fact: As of 2003, **women outnumber men** in higher paying, white collar managerial and professional occupations. Women represent 50.6% of the 48 million employees in management,*

professional and related occupations according to the Bureau of Labor Statistics.

Belief #7: There are 7 million women-owned firms in the U.S. *Fact: There are now **10.6 million** women-owned (50% or more) firms in the U.S., employing **19.1 million people** and generating **$2.5 trillion** in revenues.*

Sources for Facts 1, 2, 4, 5 and 7: Center for Women's Business Research (www.womensbusinessresearch.org). Source for 3: Small Business Administration 6: The Washington Times, 2003.

These facts, which belie the misconceptions, make it clear that women in business make up an increasingly important demographic profile for businesses to target. That being the case, allow me to pose an important question to you: Are you reaching these women in business? Do you believe that you know, for certain, how to capture your share of this important and rapidly growing market? Are you in fact even *aiming* your marketing and promotional efforts at them in the most effective ways? If you answered no to any of my questions, you can be sure that you are missing 50% of the available market for your goods and services.

Let me say that again: You are missing *half* of your potential customers, and great ones at that.

My purpose in this book is to show you how to engage this powerful market—and not with experimental tactics that may or may not work, but with *proven* strategies. Make no mistake: women are changing the way companies manufacture, design and market most of the products and services sold today. You need these customers—and they need you. It is all a matter of connecting the *right* way.

I know this for many reasons. For one, as a serial entrepreneur who gives a lot of business to companies I believe have my best interests at heart, I *am* this market. Secondly, I've been on the advisory boards of a number of companies that wanted to reach this market. I have seen what works and what does not. That understanding, knowledge and experience led me to formulate the program I share with you throughout this book: C.R.E.A.T.E.S. – Community. Relationship. Education. Anticipate. Trust. Entertainment. Service & Support.

Much has been written on marketing to *women*, including valuable books by Faith Popcorn, Marty Barletta, Mary Lou Quinlan and a number of other groundbreakers. However, little has been written about marketing to the most influential and economically powerful part of this segment, specifically, women business owners, executives and professionals. These entrepreneurial women, business leaders and high achievers are unique. They think differently, make purchasing decisions differently, and *buy* differently than the average working or non-working woman. And—*news flash!*—these businesswomen are not swayed by traditional advertising and marketing that might conceivably work, at least to some extent, with the mass market. Yet these women are especially critical for you to reach because they buy for both their businesses *and* their homes.

Are your company's products and/or services even being *noticed* by this vital market? If they are not being noticed by them, or by enough of them, you really need to know about my seven-step strategy because it will dramatically improve your ability to capture these affluent decision-makers.

I know this market like the back of my hand. As I said, I *am* this market. In all, I have started and run five successful businesses, and I have been helping businesses market to women for almost 20 years. My five-year-old consulting firm, B2Women, still helps well-known corporations successfully market to women in business. As Andrea March described in her Introduction, she and I cofounded Women's Leadership Exchange deliberately as a national multimedia company to provide businesswomen with the knowledge, the tools, mentoring support, and access to each other that women need in order to grow their businesses, specifically above the million-dollar mark, and, as often happens, even far beyond that benchmark.

The seven-step strategy I use for my clients, one that is woven into the fabric of *everything* we do at Women's Leadership Exchange, is called **C.R.E.A.T.E.S.** This acronym stands for:

C – Community
R – Relationship
E – Education
A – Anticipate
T – Trust
E – Entertainment
S – Service and Support (which are closely aligned).

In the chapters ahead, you'll discover how companies have intelligently used this proven formula to generate and sustain business. Specifically you'll learn how:

American Express inspired *trust* by helping women business owners who could not get bank loans, and setting up other programs that support women entrepreneurs to make it over that important million-dollar hurdle.

Northwestern Mutual helped build women's business *communities* that were designed around the common financial concerns of women in business.

Wyndham Hotels & Resorts *anticipated* the needs of women business travelers and also *entertains* them by offering all sorts of comforts and conveniences, both large and small, that sets them apart from other hotel chains.

IBM has long supported women's organizations, including their sponsorship of Women's Leadership Exchange. In this way, and also by actively enhancing our exposure to technology and the many practical technology solutions they offer, Big Blue shows their commitment to *community*.

...These are a few of the compelling real-life examples you'll find in these pages.

Before we move ahead, I want to make one vital point. The customer-centric C.R.E.AT.E.S. approach also resonates with many male business owners and executives! Interestingly, I have noticed that the C.R.E.A.T.E.S. formula is especially appealing to younger men, those who grew up in our changed world. These men in the younger generation are more demanding consumers than older businessmen and business owners, and are thus less likely than older males to buy solely from an advertisement or direct sales approach. Like businesswomen, these younger men understandably prefer to buy from someone whose company offers them a sense of Community, does not try to "sell to them" but builds a Relationship, Educates them, Anticipates their needs, wins their Trust, Entertains them a bit, and offers great Service and Support.

My point is that although this book is aimed at reaching businesswomen, men are *not* excluded. As you will see, if you follow my C.R.E.A.T.E.S. formula, these strategies will increase your business overall with all audiences who can use your products and services.

Dr. Sigmund Freud (1856-1939) the legendary, Austrian-born founder of psychoanalysis, once wrote: *"The great question that has never been answered, and which I have not yet been able to answer, despite my thirty years of research into the feminine soul, is 'What does a woman want?'"* From our experience we believe we can answer that question for Dr. Freud and for the world at large: Today, and perhaps this has always been the case, women want what is in short supply—more time, more peace of mind, more feeling of accomplishment. The company that creates (C.R.E.A.T.E.S.) this for them will earn their deep appreciation and allegiance.

Are you ready to learn precisely how to give your customers—past, present and future—what they want? Read on......

Chapter 2

C is for Community
Engaging Women in Communities They Trust and in Your Own 'Club'

> *"Wherever groups of women come together to define their own visions...and make connections with other groups of women...we are affirming a network of change. We are building the future."*
>
> ~Blanche Weisen Cook (1946-)
> contemporary American scholar, biographer of
> Eleanor Roosevelt

It feels like I have been an entrepreneur all my life, so much so that I sometimes think my blood is type E. But, of course, I have had the experience of working for other people, which I believe is important. Right after graduation from George Washington University, where I majored in psychology and minored in business, I moved to New York City and got my first job. It was at AIRCO, a chemical and plastics company. I had the lofty title of "Administrative Assistant to the Director of Advertising." After a couple of years there, I got my second job at Longchamps, which was then a major restaurant chain, as assistant to both the Directors of Advertising and Public Relations. Being me, I had to do my own thing. So, while I was at Longchamps, I also took on a freelance account, which was

Shun Lee Dynasty, Shun Lee Palace and Hunan, the first Szechuan and Hunan Chinese restaurants in the country. When my public relations boss left Longchamps, I was so convinced of my extraordinary marketing skills that I brazenly marched in and asked the President of Longchamps to make me Director of PR. After he got over his shock, not surprisingly, he said no. Since he now knew I was not content in my supportive position, I had to go! That led to my opening my first firm, Leslie Grossman Communications, at the age of 23.

For this budding entrepreneur, my first and greatest inspiration was my dad. He owned a furniture store and was a self-described "marketing madman," way before Crazy Eddie and his ilk. Dad ran full-page ads in the daily newspaper in York, Pennsylvania, where I grew up, with a brilliant branding ploy. In all the ads, he called himself "Dog Face Jack." I'm not sure exactly where he got that name from, but I do know that dog-face was a World War II term, and that my dad was a tail gunner in the Air Force. Nonetheless, his customers seemed to know what it meant; people from all over York County came in to buy furniture from Dog Face Jack. Overall, he was quite a guy! I naturally saw that Dad worked long hours, and likewise recognized that what he did was far from easy. But I also observed, especially as I got older, that by owning the business, humble as it was, he remained in control of his own destiny.

My mother, Charlotte, was my inspiration in another important way. When she was single, she had served as the advertising director of Stardust Lingerie, located in the Empire State Building in NYC. It was the Victoria's Secret of its time. Right after World War II, Mom married Dad and they moved to York, where he started his business. Although Mom was mostly a homemaker, she did have her own radio show for a few years called "Chatter with Charlotte." She had an incredible personality, was very smart and always advocated equal opportunities and status for women in all areas of life.

I didn't understand the influence my parents' careers had on my life until recently. Now, with a grown son and daughter of my own, both of them trying to make their way in the world, I understand the full impact both my parents had on me in terms of my professional interests and choices.

Socially, I was always outgoing—a lot like my parents—and frankly, I really liked taking charge. I guess people recognized that because I was elected president of several clubs and organizations. I also always worked after school. The odd jobs I took on in middle school and high school included everything from addressing envelopes to selling baby clothes at Sears. Then, during college, I worked as a marketing assistant at the American Psychological Association and later did a turn at a marketing firm.

After college, as my entrepreneurial career grew, I began to discover women's business associations. I saw how they provide excellent support for women on so many different levels. In addition to inspiring their members through talks and seminars, I recognized the awesome power of *networking*. In my case, networking has personally garnered me many great business leads. I picked up both Saab Cars and the BBC as clients through referrals from women with whom I networked. I also learned that the more you give, the more you receive, and regularly offered other women business owners and executives help and leads. As an active member of business associations, I made a number of lifelong friends, and they became part of my extended "community." These experiences also laid the foundation for C.R.E.A.T.E.S. and for Women's Leadership Exchange.

All the businesses I have run in my life (all five of them) have been centered on my special area of expertise, which is marketing and, in particular, how companies can best market their products and services to women. Over the years I created marketing and public relations campaigns for such women-targeted brands as Almay cosmetics, Swatch Watch, The Gap and the Platinum Guild International (PGI), among others.

Traveling the country working with accomplished women in these and other companies, I discovered that women in business were indeed a unique phenomenon, distinct from the larger mass market of "women." In 1998, my firm, CMA, was hired by Richard D'Ambrosio, then Director of Public Affairs for American Express's Small Business Services Group, which subsequently became OPEN from American Express. OPEN is now WLE's presenting sponsor. My assignment for this client was to identify marketing opportunities that would reach women business owners. The work I did for Richard led me to start the B2Women division of CMA. Later, after I sold CMA, I spun B2Women into a separate consultancy, one that I still run.

That is my background—which brings us to the first part of the C.R.E.A.T.E.S. program, *C for Community.* Supporting businesswomen and women business owners in Community is about Commitment and Connection. It is precisely within these business communities that women participate that corporations have an unparalleled opportunity to *connect* with them and show their *commitment.* "Community" can also mean that your company actually creates your *own* business community, one that will provide businesswomen with a sense of belonging.

Women hunger for real-world, in-person communities. Why? Because the lives of women business owners and women professionals are so incredibly full that, paradoxically, we often feel isolated. If that sounds strange, consider that because we are so focused on achieving our goals, we often try to do it all—keep up with our deadlines and demands at work, meet the needs of our families, take care of our homes and pets, and find the time to eat right, exercise and stay healthy. We *do* want to reach out for help and support, but do not always know where to find it. Or if we *do* know where to find that help, we often can't—or let's face it, *think* we can't—spare the time, or perhaps don't know how to ask for what we need.

Speaking of being time-starved, please allow me a digression here on multitasking. Just because we CAN multitask doesn't mean we SHOULD. Women business owners are, I think, the worst offenders. I should know. Not only am I one of these multitaskers, I'm surrounded by *thousands* of others like me at our conferences. We get in traffic accidents or have many close calls while we drive, eat breakfast in the car and make business or personal calls on our cell phones, all while we worry about being late for the meeting or think about how we're going to close the sale with the customer or client we're about to meet. At our desks, we spill coffee on our computers while we're on a conference call and at the same time doing e-mail. The people on the other end of the call hear us typing on the keyboard (the sound of the keys is magnified on the speakerphone) and know we're multitasking. Naturally they are insulted because they know you are not really listening when you are multitasking, which means you may blow the deal and the relationship. I'm no angel, but I'm working hard these days to do only two things at a time instead of five! As a result, I am less stressed, and my relationships with family, friends and colleagues have definitely improved!

Even when we do make a conscious effort to slow down and do one (or two) things at a time, we "jugglers" still find it difficult to stay in touch with friends, let alone make new ones. It is just as difficult for us to keep up with all our business contacts. Besides trying to do too much, many of us are perfectionists, so we are never satisfied or able to fully "let go." The bottom line is that there just never seems to be enough time, and we all have the same 24/7 to work with.

Think about this in your own life. What are you juggling? And do *you* ever feel frustrated when you want to talk to someone, a friend, relative or colleague or you have a pressing business issue, and wish you had someone you could discuss it with? Perhaps it's one of those days when you reach voicemail with every person you call, and then the moment passes. Where's our support network when we need it? They are probably as time-starved as you are—even as they want to reach out to you as well.

A great many of the traditional structures that used to provide support are gone, especially on a personal level. Maybe we've moved away from the people who formed our network of family and friends and no longer have helpful parents, aunts, uncles or siblings nearby, or even friendly neighbors. Gone for many, if not most of us, is the small town "where everyone knows your name." It is a significant loss.

Human beings are social creatures that, in our deepest long-ings, crave community. Anyone who doubts this should ponder how the Internet has crept into our lives. Even five years ago, none of us were sending dozens or even *hundreds* of e-mails a week (for some, a *day*) to friends, bosses, colleagues, potential dates and mates. Nor were many of us joining online special interest groups and communities, talking to strangers who were likewise gourmet foodies, pet lovers, cancer survivors, young professionals with children, new parents, buyers and sellers, collectors, etc., and receiving often instant answers to our messages. Before the Internet, we actually saw people face-to-face or called them on the telephone much more often than we do now.

While the Internet can be a great help in many ways, let's face the reality that it has also become yet another time-intensive chore that adds to our lengthy to-do list. And this, in its own way, adds to our isolation. The Internet is wonderful in many ways as a means of instant communication, yet it can also be exasperating and sometimes hazardous. Women in business, especially, often overuse it. I call the Internet, and in particular e-mail, an "extreme communications tool!" What does this mean for a business? If any company, whether they are an Internet company per se or have an Internet component, does not also have a human component, they are missing out big time. Your Web site can and must be user-friendly and helpful for your women customers. But keep in mind that you should not allow it to replace face-to-face (or voice-to-voice) contact. That is a common mistake companies make!

Community is a powerful thing. Everyone wants to feel they *belong*. Anything a company can do to actively participate in or offer women a safe community, a place where we can ask each other questions, bond and seek mutual support, will win that company the loyalty of women in business.

The question to ponder here is: How can your company help this frantically busy businesswoman? Answer that question, and you'll have that woman appreciatively on your side.

If you are not clear how Community will help your brand, consider these two facts:

(1) 70% of women believe they learn the most about a new product from a person who already owns it. (Source: Yankelovich)

(2) Women are three times more apt than men are to recommend brands when they know their friends are looking for a specific product or service. (Source: The Intuition Group)

We've found that women business owners and professionals that are active in professional associations are particularly good at sharing information, referrals and recommendations, so you want to be right there with them, in those organizations, or in one you have created for them.

Find Business Communities That Women Trust: the OPEN Story

In the past, companies thought they could become part of a community by sponsoring an event. However, sponsorship is actually just the first step in building credibility within a business community. Sponsoring women's business associations, conferences and the like *is* valuable. However, again, it is the first, albeit important, step in acquiring the customer. The second part of the equation, as I will keep stressing, is to directly engage with the customer. We need to know you, and not just as a name and a logo. We need to meet you and "feel the love." Companies that "talk the talk" are not as effective as those who also "walk the walk."

OPEN from American Express is a perfect example of a company that went to the trouble of "walking the walk" in order to engage with existing communities of women business owners. Back in 1997, OPEN (then known as "American Express Small Business Services") initiated its first foray into marketing to women in business by becoming a sponsor of the National Association of Women Business Owners - New York City

Chapter (NAWBO-NYC) and also sending their executives to NAWBO meetings to increase their visibility and find out first-hand what their customers need and want.

OPEN had examined the statistics, were able to clearly recognize that the number of women business owners in the U.S. was rapidly growing into a powerful market, and knew that test-marketing to this audience on a grassroots level would give them a substantial "focus group" and market advantage. Starting quietly and modestly, they began to build credibility in the New York metropolitan area, which was and is one of their key markets.

Sharon Emek, who at that time owned the largest women-owned insurance agency in the New York metropolitan area, was then president of NAWBO-NYC. She approached OPEN on behalf of NAWBO and agreed to encourage American Express Business Card memberships. For their part, OPEN agreed that whenever a NAWBO member acquired an American Express Card, a set part of the fee would go back to help the chapter. In this winning formula, OPEN showed that their company wanted to reward the networking organization for its member-ship's support of OPEN, while they also helped fuel the growth of women-owned businesses.

Another way OPEN gradually built credibility as a company that supports and is truly interested in the needs of women business owners was by initiating newsworthy surveys about women business owners. These survey results, which compared the similarities and differences between female- and male-owned businesses, were announced to the media jointly with NAWBO-NYC. These surveys showed unequivocally that increasing numbers of women were now running businesses in fields traditionally owned by men (for example, in construction and manufacturing) and that female/male uses of capital and even size of businesses were often the same. The surveys likewise showed that female- and male-owned businesses were beginning to *look* alike. The ensuing publicity garnered attention for the American Express card as a desirable tool for small business owners, and helped raise public awareness of the New York City Chapter of NAWBO. While I was president of NAWBO's New York City Chapter from 1999 to 2000, OPEN continued as a major NAWBO-NYC sponsor. As positive results snowballed, OPEN increased their investment in this networking organization.

In 2002, when Andrea and I designed Women's Leadership Exchange, we proposed to Kerry Hatch, the then-CEO of OPEN, that they "take their show on the road." Why not build on their initial success with the NAWBO-NYC sponsorship, we suggested, and become the presenting sponsor of *our* new entity! This one could and would, we said, catapult their support of women business owners nationally as a continuing grassroots opportunity to connect with their community. What we proposed would include tremendous marketing exposure for OPEN via the Women's Leadership Exchange's regional conferences in New York, Dallas, Chicago, Southern California and Atlanta. Our conferences, we told them, would draw substantial numbers of women business owners who already had significant businesses and were looking for ways to promote their growth, which would mean, in some cases, that they could go on to far exceed a million dollars in annual sales. Thus, our expected attendees would present the perfect audiences for OPEN! In addition, we explained, our Web site could link directly to OPEN's soon-to-be-created women's initiative.

OPEN knew they both wanted and needed live, in-person contact with women business owners around the country, which would allow them to truly become part of the business communities these women already belonged to and trusted.

Kerry Hatch and other decision makers at OPEN agreed to become the presenting sponsor of WLE's national program, and soon found themselves benefiting from WLE's extensive marketing campaigns, content-rich Web site, e-newsletter, and one-to-one contact with the thousands of women business owners who attend WLE conferences.

Now under the leadership of President Susan Sobbott, OPEN from American Express has expanded its commitment to women business owners. In short order, OPEN launched a new Web site (OPEN.americanexpress.com/women) that offers a rich abundance of resources for women business owners, including articles on surviving cash flow crunches, effective marketing and sales, how to find financing, advice on hiring staff, how to apply for business credit cards, credit line information and much, much more. The OPEN community Web site now also offers informative surveys, such as a recent one that shows that 66% of women business owners are likely to take a substantial or above average financial risk when investing for their businesses. This survey was conducted by the Center for Women's Business Research¯another women-based community resource supported by OPEN!!

WLE also proposed to OPEN that they offer WLE conference attendees special discounts as another way to demonstrate their interest in investing in the success of women business owners. Now, if a woman uses an OPEN/American Express card to pay for admission to a Women's Leadership Exchange conference, she receives a $50 discount.

OPEN, as a company, C.R.E.A.T.E.S. Community. They also utilize every other step of the seven-step program to reach its target market, including Relationship, Education, Anticipate,

Trust, Entertainment, and Service/Support.

Create Your Own Community: Northwestern Mutual

Another way to be part of a women's business community is to create one of your own for them. One such method is to form a professional women's advisory council made up of the kind of businesswomen who are your potential clients or customers. For Northwestern Mutual, a Milwaukee-based corporation, I spearheaded the creation of advisory councils in Seattle, Las Vegas, Chicago, Grand Rapids and other cities. Here's how I did it for them, and how your company can likewise form one.

As part of helping them create a Northwestern Mutual Community, I instructed Northwestern's women representatives to invite about 20 to 25 high-powered women in their geographic area, women they either knew or knew of, to breakfast or lunch. The purpose of this gathering was to allow the women to discuss their biggest concerns around financial matters. At the first meeting, before the meal began, I asked each of the women to give a two-minute introduction to everyone about who they were and what kind of business they were in. Later we went around the room again and asked them to share one major concern about money that was on their mind. The group host was a female financial representative from Northwestern Mutual. She wrote down these issues so that, at future meetings, experts could address the most common financial issues and concerns.

At a second meeting, which was held at either a restaurant or a private club, an expert would speak. Then we held a lively Q&A session. Sometimes this expert was an attorney who specialized in estate planning, or an investment advisor. A Northwestern Mutual rep for life insurance was also always there.

The results were always quite magical. At the very first meeting, the women opened up and talked about their fears, voicing some that they said they had never before confided to anyone. A number were affluent women who were recently divorced or widowed, and had discovered they had been left with far less money than they had expected. Many successful women even confessed they were afraid of ending up as "bag ladies," a not uncommon fear. A majority assumed that *other* women knew exactly how to plan for their financial futures, although they did not, and learned it wasn't true. Even women "at the top" didn't know everything, or did not have complete confidence in their financial futures.

At these meetings, attended by businesswomen of different ages and industries, the same concerns were shared across the board. In a Michigan women's advisory council I helped form, for example, one attendee, a woman in her early 30's, owned a retail flower store. There was also an advertising agency owner in her early 40's, a mother-and-daughter pair (a woman who owned several restaurants with her 30-something daughter), two female lawyers (one with a big firm, the other with her own practice), a health care company owner in her 60's, a hospital executive in her 40's, a PR agency owner in her 40's, and a woman who co-owned an accounting firm with her husband and had two offices, one in Michigan, the other in Texas. Interestingly, I recognized that woman because she had attended a WLE conference in Dallas—it is a small world! Usually, there is also at least one woman who owns her own real estate brokerage firm.

I am always moved by what happens at these advisory council meetings.Women who once felt isolated now find themselves in a safe place where they can be educated about financial issues, and most of them feel comfortable asking questions without feeling embarrassed. There is also the bonus of networking with some 20 other businesswomen from many different fields, people they might ordinarily not get to meet.

I usually fly in to facilitate each advisory council's first meeting. After that, the meetings develop a life of their own as the group continues to meet quarterly throughout the year. The group also becomes self-sustaining and nurturing as the women develop a bond with each other. Together, the women decide which financial issues are most important to them and engage different speakers from the host company's network, or from their own areas, to address and help them resolve common issues of concern. Along the way, these women learn to appreciate and use the tools and services provided by the sponsor firm—which could be *you*.

An important distinction: because the women at these informative and interesting breakfast or lunch meetings don't feel they are being sold to, most of them do end up doing business with or referring friends to the host company, which in this case was Northwestern Mutual, a company that certainly lives up to the "Mutual" in its name!

IBM: Big Blue – A Big Friend to Women Business Owners
Many, if not most, women entrepreneurs have embraced technology as the essential business tool it is. Technology allows us to multitask like crazy, helps us reduce our overhead expenses, enables us to be more competitive, and, best of all, helps us grow bigger, more profitable businesses with ease. In fact, women-owned firms with over $1 million in sales are more likely than their male counterparts to embrace technology as an integral part of their business strategy (58% vs. 35%). In addition, these women-owned firms are also more apt to have a Web site with transactional capability—56% vs. 38%. (Statistics are

from Center for Women's Business Research.) Thus, it is wonderfully appropriate that a company like IBM is and has actively focused on women in business since 1992.

IBM has long supported women's business organizations. This includes NAWBO, NAFE (National Association of Female Executives), WPO (Women Presidents' Organization) and the American Business Women's Association, to name a few. IBM has also been active in various educational efforts; for example, they support the Center for Women's Business Research (who conducted the survey I referred to above). They also offer scholarships for women to study engineering. Plus, they sponsor WLE conferences. The company offers WLE Keyholders technology discounts and reduced rates for leasing or purchasing IBM laptops.

This year, IBM launched a terrific Web site for technology solutions aimed at small to mid-sized businesses, the IBM Express Portfolio (http://express-portfolio.com/ibm). There, IBM provides answers to, or offers suggestions for, such business challenges as how to analyze information for better decision-making, how to improve your customers' experience, and how to increase your flexibility in the face of market volatility. This kind of support is great for us maddeningly busy business owners because it allows us to improve our responsiveness to customers, suppliers and strategic partners, and helps us streamline our business procedures in general.

A great deal of the credit for IBM's nurturing involvement with businesswomen, particularly women business owners, must go to the perceptive vision of Patti Ross, IBM's Market Segment Executive, Women Entrepreneurs, and the able leadership of Marilyn Johnson, IBM's dynamic Vice President for Market Development.

Marilyn, by the way, is simply a powerhouse. She has been with IBM for 28 years and travels the same circuit I do. Interestingly, Marilyn and I attend many of the same conferences, and met recently in Mexico City at the Global Women's Summit, where 900 businesswomen from 90 countries convened. IBM just announced that they are taking their marketing to businesswomen global...and guess who made the announcement and is spearheading the initiative? Yes, Marilyn Johnson and Patti Ross! Kudos to you both, and to IBM, for reaching out to women worldwide!

I am honored to tell you that we offered Marilyn the role of Chair of the newly formed WLE Multicultural Advisory Board and she accepted. The mission of this body is to discover what all businesswomen want and need, be they Latina, African-American, Asian, Native American or from other cultures with unique challenges. Our Board consists of women from all these groups, and they are helping us uncover what these challenges are, and how we can help these women grow their businesses into the multimillions. I am certain that Marilyn's vision and leadership will play a major role in the success of this initiative.

Case Study:
eBay: It's All About the Community

The online auction giant, eBay, is one company that has built a passionately dedicated and enthusiastic worldwide community from scratch—an astonishingly successful coup—and become a household name, the ultimate triumph in corporate branding! With $4 billion in revenues and an astounding 70% three-year growth rate (ranked #8 on *Fortune* Magazine's "Fastest-Growing Companies" list in 2004), eBay has created a community of women and men, buyers and sellers of everything from clothing, collectibles, cars and jewelry to antiques and fine art.

It's not just "selling stuff from your basement." Major retailers from IBM and Sears to Sharper Image sell overstocked inventory on eBay. It's also not just local, it's global: international sales constituted a whopping 46% of eBay's total sales in the second quarter of 2004.

The company's formula is shockingly simple: eBay itself neither buys nor sells products or services, but instead provides an online marketplace where people come together to buy or sell any imaginable item. The company collects a listing fee, plus a small commission on each item sold. Nearly 500,000 full- and part-time entrepreneurs sell products on eBay. Many are "Power Sellers" who sell over $10,000 in products each month. Others make a living as eBay brokers, representing sellers who don't want to be bothered with the details of listing their products or monitoring the online auctions. Now eBay represents "the most explosive opportunity for retailers ever," short of the franchising industry boom in the 1950's and 60's, says Rieva Lesonsky, editor-at-large of *Entrepreneur* Magazine. The magazine even published a special "eBay Startup Guide" for readers in a joint venture with eBay. *Entrepreneur*, by the way, is also a Women's Leadership Exchange media partner, and published a Special Edition magazine for women business owners called "The Exchange," which was inspired by WLE. This publication was a big hit!

The fascinating success of eBay is an illuminating textbook example for any corporation interested in building an online community. They did it by involving people from all walks of life, even complete strangers living in every state in the U.S. and in other countries across the globe. It should come as no surprise that eBay's CEO is a woman, Meg Whitman, and that in 2004 Meg was named one of *Fortune's* "50 Most Powerful Women in Business." Although Meg Whitman wasn't a founder of eBay, she is a Harvard Business School-educated, seasoned corporate executive, who spent years building brands for Procter & Gamble, Disney, Hasbro, StrideRite and Bain Consulting. Meg was brought in by eBay founder Pierre Omidyar to lead his small start-up, which began as his notion of how he could help his girlfriend build her collection of Pez dispensers!

Interestingly, Whitman constantly refers to eBay's "community" to account for its astounding success. As quoted in a 2003 *Fortune Magazine* 2003 profile, "Meg and the Machine," Whitman notes, "This company truly is built by the community of users." Whitman also believes in *listening* to her community, who e-mail her in droves. She also makes every possible effort to connect eBay users to each other, and, when meeting individual users in person is approachable and unpretentious, with a folksy, down-home manner.

At annual meetings called *eBay Live,* where about 10,000 people gather, Whitman, instead of wearing the expected power suit, generally wears an eBay shirt. Talk about living your brand! As she autographs and hands out trading cards of herself and other eBay leaders—which is better than a business card and collectible, to boot—she tells attendees: "We succeed when you succeed." That statement in itself is one of the most customer-centric things any CEO can say!

Way back in her Procter & Gamble brand manager days, Whitman wrote in her journal about what she believes is important: "It's all about the customer." Tom Tierney, Whitman's ex-boss at Bain, and now an eBay board member, once paid her the ultimate compliment about the loyalty of eBay's customers when he said, as reported in *Fortune*: "It felt to me almost more like a movement than a business."

Case Study:
Weight Watchers: Bonding Over Pounds – Weigh to Go!
Weight Watchers International (WW) is a company that has long proven itself a big winner at making people "big losers." A 2005 recent survey shows that WW is the only weight loss program proven to help people not only lose weight but successfully maintain the loss, which is a big deal since that is often the most difficult part. A University of Pennsylvania study of the nation's 10 most popular diet programs found that people in Weight Watchers lost about 5% of their weight in six months (about 10 pounds) and kept about half of it off for two years. Modest as this might seem, it is a major accomplishment—and many people *do* manage to stay at their goal weight indefinitely—which also means they are a "Lifetime Member" and can come to WW meetings for free!

Since an estimated 45 million people in the U.S. diet each year, weight loss is a huge business. For most people, shedding pounds is difficult and tedious. At Weight Watchers, the "community spirit" is very strong. There participants lose weight inside a supportive community environment. Classes are composed of 95% women, but many of these members take the diet home and share it with their husbands or boyfriends.

In a smart business move, Weight Watchers now allows companies to hold sessions on-site. These weight loss meetings held in businesses are a great way for employers to show their interest in their employees' health and fitness. This support provides an important sense of community that helps women feel they are no longer alone in their weight loss struggles. Weight Watchers has also succeeded in spinning off a highly successful frozen foods line, a magazine, and numerous other brand extensions.

I personally am a big fan. I've lost the most weight I ever lost,

20 pounds, through Weight Watchers, and have kept most of it off. I formed a mini-community of weight loss support with my brother and sister-in-law (I did say mini!) and we even have our own support group at WLE headquarters. Jolene Zupnik, WLE's Relationship Manager, a beautiful young woman who hit her lifetime goal two years ago, leads it. Jolene provides us with recipes, tips and coaching that help Andrea and me, along with the entire staff, keep our weight down. I also buy the company's ice cream sandwiches and many of their other products. If there are two similar products, I will always choose their product because they have my loyalty! Weight Watchers is another fine example of a company that C.R.E.A.T.E.S. their continuing success through marketing intelligently to women.

Chapter 3

R is for Relationships:
Forming a Unique Bond with Your
Prospective Customers

*"If you want to be listened to, you should put
in time listening."*
~Marge Piercy (1936-) American poet

A s I said earlier, and it is, I think, a widely accepted fact, women who own their own businesses, and women in general, are far more likely than men to buy from companies and people with whom they have relationships. Nonetheless, most salespeople are taught to sell in what I call a "typical male model." Many insurance representatives, for example, are told to focus exclusively on financial standing, size of business and personal information to determine whether to offer them their products. But build a *relationship*? Fuggedaboutit!

Again using the insurance industry, because it offers us such a dramatic "male model" example, it's the accepted mindset in that industry that if you haven't sold a customer by the second meeting, you're probably never going to sell to him or her. And further, if that prospect is a woman, you're *really* never going to sell to her. Unbelievable, but true! In other words, insurance salespeople are taught to look at the numbers or statistics rather than at the person. They also are not helped to understand that we women do not like to feel "sold to," as if we are a predictable commodity instead of individuals. The fact is we like to feel we are being given informed choices and the opportunity to make such choices. It's a matter of respect.

Ideally, the sales process in selling an insurance policy, or *any* financial product or service, to a women business owner or executive should be a getting-to-know-you process. Most women prefer relationships to one-night stands. Why would the decisions we make in our business lives be radically different? In reality, most everything in life, in the final analysis, comes back to relationships. Admittedly, a "relationship building" selling style may take a while longer—especially if your prospect, the women business owner or executive, is extremely busy. It might take three, four or even *five* meetings to clinch the deal. However, if you invest the time and energy necessary to build a relationship, and win her trust—that's the "T" in C.R.E.A.T.E.S. which we'll talk about fully in a later chapter—not only will she buy from you, but once she feels you've taken the time to establish the basis of a relationship, she'll also reward you with referrals to good prospects in her life and work circles. And it does not get any better than good word of mouth!

Relationship-Based Selling: Northwestern Mutual
Northwestern Mutual is an example of a company that values, and makes use of, relationship-based selling. Yes, this is the same company I described in the last chapter, the one for which I organized women's advisory councils. In this instance, it was 2001, and the company's sales reps in their Seattle office needed to learn how to build relationships with women, so I helped them by training their strongest women reps in the C.R.E.A.T.E.S. strategy, one by one. After the success of that project, I was asked to train groups of both men and women

reps. I did so, traveling around the country, and in 2002 and 2003, also gave talks on the program at many of Northwestern Mutual's regional conferences.

As part of this training, every month my company, B2Women, initiated a conference call with all the Northwestern Mutual's female reps in the program. These reps, incidentally, now use the C.R.E.A.T.E.S. customer-centric style for all their prospects. This conference-call model, which we still use, is designed to allow the 12 to 15 women on the call to build relationships with their colleagues from the company who are in different parts of the country. They share what works and what does not, and then use this information to build better relationships with current and potential customers. I am on hand to offer suggestions and advice from my experience that can help them overcome any challenges. Previously, they had no support, and, not surprisingly, their customers were almost exclusively men.

This program went over like gangbusters, and, for the first time in its history, Northwestern Mutual is selling like crazy to women business owners, executives and professionals. A twelve-month pilot program we put in place in 2003 specifically targeted women professionals and women business owners. The result of that pilot program was that those reps who participated outsold their peers by 22% in life insurance premiums alone! And guess what else? The reps also outsold their peers in disability insurance, long-term care insurance—the two lead products in the women's market—and investment products, by double digits, *and* increased the number of insurance policies owned by women by 12%. Industry and third-party research shows that Northwestern Mutual now enjoys a steadily increasing brand awareness and customer satisfaction level that is much higher than many of its traditional and non-traditional competitors.

Platinum: A Girl's Best Friend?

It's interesting how things evolve. I became involved with Northwestern through Sue Tompkins, who served as Northwestern Mutual's Director of Market Development when I first met her. Sue later became the company's Director of Professional Women's Market Development. She contacted me because she had heard about a program I developed for selling platinum jewelry to women. At the time, most industries didn't view women as decision makers and purchasers, and believe it or not, the *jewelry* industry was no exception! This antiquated mindset persisted despite statistics even back then that showed beyond doubt that as much as 85% of all household purchases are, in fact, determined by women!

The seven-year public relations program I created for Platinum Guild International (PGI) targeted affluent women, including women business owners and executives. It ultimately resulted in a 700% growth in retail sales of platinum jewelry in the U.S. in the 1990's! I was then running my PR and marketing firm, Communications/Marketing Action (CMA). We had devised a program to educate jewelry manufacturers and retailers about how women think and how they make decisions, and it was very successful. When I explained the program to Sue Tompkins of Northwestern Mutual, she said it was like a light bulb going off in her head! She *got it*, made the creative leap, and believed that the same principles—understanding how women customers think and changing your sales focus to reflect that reality—would apply to her own industry, insurance. This, of course, turned out to be the case.

However, let me say that changing conventional thinking at PGI and the industry itself was far from easy. Have you noticed that nothing in life worth doing is ever easy? We had some big challenges to overcome. First of all, platinum, used in armaments, had been declared a strategic metal in World War II, so for many years it could not legally be used in the U.S. in jewelry or other kinds of products that were non-strategic. It took many years before this ban was lifted. As a result, a whole generation of American jewelers had never worked with platinum, which is rarer and more expensive than gold, and also more difficult and time-consuming to mine. Before the ban, platinum was considered the most elite metal. After the ban was lifted, reversing the trend was difficult. White gold had since been developed, and manufacturers felt that since white gold had the "look" of platinum, who needed the real thing?

Our initial objective was to convince American manufacturers and retailers that platinum was indeed going to be the Next Big Thing. We also had to show them how to work with it! An additional marketing challenge was this: conventional wisdom held that men bought jewelry for women, so almost all marketing of jewelry was directed at men. Today, of course, many if not most women have their own money and their own independence. Those of us who are self-supporting or are partners in a two-income household are no longer willing to wait for a husband or boyfriend to buy us jewelry. We can and do buy it for ourselves when we feel like it. However, this time we had our work cut out for us!

We zoomed into action right from the start to garner the attention of manufacturers and retailers. My company placed media stories in prestigious jewelry trade publications such as *National Jeweler* and *Jeweler's Quarterly*. We simultaneously promoted stories in lifestyle media that featured beautifully designed European platinum jewelry pieces, crafted by artisans in Italy and Germany. We were able to land feature coverage in such influential fashion magazines as *Vogue, W* and *Harper's Bazaar*. Affluent, trendsetting women read the articles, saw the photographs, and wanted the jewelry. We also arranged special events. For example, we held an elegant party at the Italian Trade Commission in New York, to which we invited high-level jewelry manufacturers and retailers. One of the highlights of this sparkling event was a concert featuring a musician whose instrument was a platinum flute!

Back on the media front, we convinced fashion editors that the next big trend was platinum jewelry, and that women going to jewelry stores would be asking for platinum jewelry, and would buy it for themselves! This is known as a classic push-pull strategy. When customers come into their stores and ask for something they want that the store does not carry, smart retailers will go to manufacturers and order what customers are asking them for. This is a big part of what happened with platinum: we created a multifaceted action plan, and put it in place to create product demand on multiple fronts. Eventually, everything fell into place beautifully.

Recently, I saw a jewelry advertisement geared to women that jolted me into once again realizing how far we've come. The campaign was for a new "diamond right-hand ring" from the diamond industry. Printed in the *Conde Nast Traveler*, the ad copy read: "Your left hand loves candlelight. Your right hand loves the spotlight. Your left hand declares your commitment. Your right hand is a declaration of independence. Women of the world, raise your right hand." I nearly fell off my chair. Bravo, DeBeers! And bravo, women of the world, for loving and honoring yourselves rather than waiting for Prince Charming to buy you what you want and deserve! Nonetheless, this sure wasn't true back then!

Microsoft Enters the Picture...
Microsoft is one of the most successful companies in the tech-

nology business and shares the world stage with IBM as one of the two most powerful technology brands on the planet. Microsoft has also long targeted small business. However, in 2004 they began to become more aware of the strength and market promise of yet another market—the *women* business owner market. I had the privilege of presenting the C.R.E.A.T.E.S. strategy to their small business team, headed by Cindy Bates, Microsoft U.S. Small Business Manager, at a LIVE Meeting, which is a Microsoft Web conferencing service. This meeting was arranged by Aaron Bernstein, Microsoft's Director of Strategic Alliances and Partnerships.

I am happy to say that only a month or so after that Live Meeting, Aaron called and related that Microsoft wanted to get their feet wet in the women business owner market. The upshot for me, in what was a classic win-win formula (don't you just love them?) for Microsoft, WLE and our Keyholders, was that Microsoft became a sponsor of Women's Leadership Exchange. As I've said earlier, corporate sponsors can directly jumpstart their outreach programs and introduce new products and services by activating the B2Women C.R.E.A.T.E.S. strategy at WLE conferences.

Microsoft's initial sponsorship of the WLE 2004 conference in New York City put Aaron and the Microsoft Small Business Group directly in front of more than 800 women business owners on that one day alone.

In one fell swoop, Microsoft earned a C for Community and an R for Relationship. The company became part of a live community at the conference and an Internet community at WLE's Web site (www.womensleadershipexchange.com) with links directly to Microsoft's online Small Business Center.

For Microsoft, C in the equation is particularly important, since many people, and I would have to say women in particular, still view Microsoft as a behemoth company, too big to care about women business owners. Since women like to buy from companies that care (which we'll explore in detail in Chapter Eight: S is for Service and Support), Microsoft's communal relationship with them via WLE has begun to change this perception. Microsoft is now demonstrating their commitment to educating (E-Education) women business owners (WBO) on how they can save time and money by using Microsoft products. That educational program will also earn Microsoft a T for Trust.

After seeing such positive results at the first WLE conference they sponsored, Microsoft decided to go into the WBO market in a big way. They did this by setting up a separate section of their online small business center for women business owners (www.microsoft.com/womeninbusiness). Based on their initial success, they signed on as a National Corporate Partner for WLE. This relationship affords the company a face-to-face presence at WLE's five regional conferences around the country and a year-long web presence on our Web site. They are also exploring other opportunities to carry out the C.R.E.A.T.E.S. strategy so that they employ all seven steps!

Microsoft may be in the infancy of their marketing effort to this hot new market, but they clearly recognize it for what it is and have begun to capture it in a big way. Congratulations, Microsoft, you're off to a very smart start!

Case Study:
Starbucks: It's Not About the Coffee
It may sound like my mantra, but I have to say it again because it cannot be overemphasized: women like to do business with the individuals, companies and brands that we can count on to

always be there for us when we need them. Starbucks is one of those rare brands that beautifully illustrates and fulfills this prerequisite. The company has done a remarkable job of creating a relationship between a brand and its customers, which is not an easy thing for a retail establishment to do. It isn't only about the coffee, although their coffee is delicious. After all, we don't have a relationship with Dunkin' Donuts, and they also sell coffee!

How on earth did Starbucks, which is now ranked number one on *Fortune* Magazine's "Ten Most Admired Companies" list in the Products and Services category, accomplish this? Let's start with *cozy*. Starbucks stores are designed to feel comfortable and "living room-like." For people in small city apartments or busy homes, their local Starbucks is often their home away from home where they can relax over a cup of coffee, read the paper, work on their computers, meet a friend or business associate, or just be with people when they feel isolated.

This atmosphere and business philosophy stands conventional wisdom on its head—since most restaurants and cafes in the U.S. think quick turnover is the key to profit. At Starbucks, no one rushes you or pressures you to leave to make room for new customers. That attitude builds customer loyalty for a lot more than a Latte Grande or a Caramel Macchiato. And customer loyalty builds customer retention. While many restaurants and cafes struggle to attract new customers, Starbucks does all it can to keep existing customers by turning their coffeehouses into social centers.

I've been to Starbucks stores in New York, Los Angeles, Seattle, Boston and Greenwich, Connecticut. Wherever the store is, however, the atmosphere is always the same, and always encourages you to feel comfortable. Starbucks even offers wireless access for laptops and personal digital assistants (PDAs).

Because customers feel so connected to Starbucks, they don't mind paying what many consider a high price for a cup of coffee or the pastries, sandwiches and other items they sell. Recently, I bought a CD at Starbucks. Yes, a CD! Sure, you can purchase a CD at a music store, or a newspaper at a newsstand, or coffee makers at a department or kitchenware store, or a sandwich or salads at a deli, and so on. But you don't have to— you can get all these items at *Starbucks*. What busy person doesn't love easy, convenient one-stop-shopping in a cozy atmosphere? Because the chain *anticipated* and provided for all these needs, Starbucks is another an excellent example of "A is for Anticipates" in our C.R.E.A.T.E.S. strategy.

A word about service: I have consistently been treated warmly and enthusiastically by Starbucks "baristas," the people who make and sell the products. They are clearly exceptionally well-trained to treat customers as if they are good friends. Maybe these employees are always smiling because their employer is on *Fortune's* "100 Best Companies to Work For" list.

Sponsoring your own events works...

Companies that sponsor their own events will build relationships *between* customers, will build relationships *with* existing customers, and will attract *new* customers through word-of-mouth—also known as "creating a buzz." Remember that 70% of women learn about a new product from someone who already owns or uses one, and also that women are three times more likely than men to recommend brands when they know their family member, friend or business associate is seeking a specific product or service, as I mentioned earlier. You *want* women to talk to each other about you...in a positive light of course! And again, please keep in mind that men also appreciate a relationship-based, customer-centric approach.

Relationships are one of the strongest, if not *the* strongest part of the C.R.E.A.T.E.S. program for marketing your business. These seven essential marketing strategies, both individually and cumulatively, are what C.R.E.A.T.E.S. enduring relationships with customers!

Chapter 4

E is for Education
Helping Your Customers Succeed By
Expanding Their Knowledge

> *"If you have knowledge, let others light their candles in it."*
>
> ~Margaret Fuller (1810-1850)
> US Transcendentalist author, editor & lecturer

Businesswomen put great value on education and trust companies that invest in them by providing it. Why? Because women in business are hungry for information. Please don't pressure us to buy. Instead, "feed" us by educating us about your products or services, and how they can positively impact our lives and our success. Tell us the benefits. Compare the differences from other, similar products. Explain how yours will make our lives or our businesses easier. Also, show us how they actually work, in detail, and describe related trends that fit into the bigger picture. Give us information we can't easily get elsewhere, and we will begin to fall in love with you!

Going above and beyond, investing the extra time and effort to educate a woman customer shows her—shows all of us—that your company truly cares about her and her business. Companies that help women learn without "hard-selling" us will score points and build credibility. This is true even if the information you provide does not always directly relate to your products or services. Whatever you do, never talk down to us. We are busy, but we are also smart and eager to learn what we don't know, or what we may not even know we don't know until you tell us or show us!

The Census Bureau reports that women now make up 56% of all college students in the U.S. In fact, women have constituted the majority of college students in the U.S. since 1979. And, since education is a key factor in higher earnings, this trend has several important repercussions. For one thing, the proportion of women who earn more than their husbands or potential spouses will increase to unprecedented levels, says Harvard labor economist Richard B. Freeman, author of *The Feminization of Work in the USA: A New Era of (Man) Kind?*

This hunger to learn on the part of women means that we are more apt than men to seek advice from advisors, colleagues, friends and others when we make a purchase or other decision. However, we often just don't have enough time for these fact and opinion gathering consultations. That's why women use the Internet so frequently for research purposes. We use it to educate ourselves about all kinds of things, including health, real estate, investments, travel, college admissions and scholarships for our children, and for price comparisons, to name just a few areas.

Anthropologist Helen Fisher, author of *The First Sex,* says women "gather more details around them...and they tend to weigh more variables, consider more options and find multiple solutions." Hey, back in the cave days, we women were the gatherers even then! The point is women want to have what they consider sufficient information to make any decision, whether it's personal or business-related.

(L) to (R): Andrea March, Cofounder, WLE; 2005 Compass Award winner, Gloria Allred, leading women's rights attorney; Anne Robinson, General Counsel, American Express; Leslie Grossman, Cofounder, WLE

(L) to (R): Leslie Grossman, Cofounder, WLE; Anne Robinson, Group Counsel, American Express; 2005 WLE/OPEN Compass Award winners Harriet Michel, President, National Minority Supplier Development Council and Suzanne de Passe, CEO, de Passe Entertainment; Sylvia Gomez, CBS 2 Chicago; and Andrea March, Cofounder, WLE

Cindy Bates, General Manager, US Small Business, for Microsoft, with Jane Fonda and Gloria Steinem at WLE New York.

Sophia Corona, CFO, Bigfoot Interactive, (right) greets Keynoter Pernille Spiers-Lopez, President, IKEA North America, in the WLE Interactive Information Center in Southern California.

Politicians and other leaders are drawn to women business owners. Here Leslie meets with NYC Mayor Michael Bloomberg at Gracie Mansion.

(L) to (R): Penni Berns, VP, High Value Customer Relationship Management, OPEN from American Express; 2004 WLE/OPEN Compass Award winner Cicely Tyson; Gail Evans, author and former EVP, CNN

WLE Growth Guru Orit, President and CEO, The O Group, leads a marketing seminar at WLE Dallas.

WLE Keynoter Gloria Steinem addresses nearly 800 women business owners at WLE New York.

WLE Cofounders Leslie Grossman and Andrea March greet women business owners in the general session at WLE Dallas.

Alexa Brownell Reese, Director, Advocacy Marketing for OPEN from American Express meets with women business owners at the WLE Interactive Information Center.

An emotional moment for Jane Fonda as she is awarded the prestigious WLE Vanguard Award in New York.

Women business owners around the Office Depot booth in the Interactive Information Center at WLE Dallas 2005.

(L) to (R): WLE/OPEN Compass Award winners for Dallas 2005: Lupe Valdez, first woman Sheriff of Dallas County; Catherine Crier, Court-TV anchor; Dr. Lorraine Monroe, Founder, the Lorraine Monroe Leadership Institute

Actress Marlo Thomas greets attendees and signs her book in the Interactive Information Center at WLE Dallas 2005.

(L) to (R): Leslie Grossman, Cofounder, WLE; Marlo Thomas, actress, author and philanthropist; Cary Broussard, VP Marketing, Women On Their Way, Wyndham Hotels and Resorts; Judy Hendrick, EVP and Chief Investment Officer, Wyndham Hotels and Resorts

(L) to (R): Leslie Grossman, Cofounder, WLE; Marilyn Johnson, VP Market Development, IBM; WLE Compass Award winner Carolyn Kepcher, EVP, The Trump Organization; Caroline Gundeck, First VP Multicultural & Diversified Business Development Director, Women's Market Advisory Division, Merrill Lynch; Andrea March, Cofounder, WLE

WLE Cofounders Leslie Grossman and Andrea March open the 2005 WLE conference in Southern California.

(L) to (R): Leslie Grossman, Cofounder, WLE; Aaron Bernstein, Director, Strategic Alliances & Partnerships, Microsoft; WLE Keynoter and past WLE/OPEN Compass Award winner Suzanne de Passe, CEO, de Passe Entertainment; Anne Robinson, General Counsel, American Express; Andrea March, Cofounder, WLE

Women business owners meet with sponsors at the WLE Interactive Information Center in Southern California.

Gloria Steinem, women's rights leader, activist and author, acknowledges women business owners at the WLE New York 2004 Conference.

(L) to (R): Leslie Grossman, Cofounder, WLE; Marilyn Johnson, VP of Market Development, IBM; Andrea March, Cofounder, WLE; 2005 WLE/OPEN Compass Award winners Dr. Cheryl Shavers, Founder and CEO, Global Smarts, Inc., Former Under Secretary of Commerce for Technology; and Doris Christopher, Founder, The Pampered Chef, flank the IBM booth in the WLE Interactive Information Center.

How to Educate Your Customers – Talks, Classes, Demos, Newsletters

There are many ways you can educate your customer. These multimedia channels include conferences, seminars or webinars (another name for online conferences), workshops, one-to-one meetings, brochures, newsletters, e-newsletters, or your all-important Web site. If you're a bank, investment brokerage firm or insurance company, you might want to offer talks, classes or a breakfast or lunch meeting to educate businesswomen about money. If you do the latter, please try to not make the mistake many financial services firms make. They schedule one-time seminars and send their representatives there with orders to close sales on the spot. Women who attend these kinds of high pressure events often feel scammed. Once trust is broken, it's tough to rebuild it. Remember Northwestern Mutual's women's advisory councils and the terrific results they achieved with them in creating community and building relationships. Educating your prospective client/customer is not about putting the squeeze on them.

Here are some other ideas: if you're a retailer, you can offer how-to seminars on issues related to your products. This is what Lowe's, the home improvement chain, does with its how-to clinics. Or you can host in-store shows, kids' play areas, and after-hours parties, as some electronics and active wear retailers do. Use your imagination in order to take a more proactive stance to help your potential customers and make the buying experience pleasurable and worthwhile. It will bring your customers closer to you, and—be patient—it will also impact favorably on your bottom line.

A newsletter can be a great educational tool. You will need to gear it to your audience, customizing it for their distinct point of view. To focus *your* newsletter, you need to know who your readers are likely to be and what they want and need. Whether you deliver the newsletter to them in print or as an e-newsletter is not the most important point. The main point is that your readers are made to feel that their specific needs and interests are being addressed. For example, WLE's e-newsletter is tailored to women business owners, and everything we cover in it reflects that orientation. By the way, if you'd like to be on our e-mail list to receive "The Exchange," please let us know. It's free!

Case Study:
Lowe's: Improving Your Life, Not Just Your Home

Lowe's has done an especially good job of educating its customers, and potential customers, on how to use its tools and equipment. For one thing, they offer free how-to clinics on everything from faux paint finishes to closet organization systems. The library on its Web site, likewise offered at no cost, presents visitors with an absolute treasure trove of creative ideas, cost calculators and tools on such topics as home décor, flooring, lighting/electrical, lawn and garden, paint and home organization. If you're planning a move, they offer an in-depth section that thoughtfully includes everything you need to consider before and after moving—including a mortgage payment calculator, city profiles and a cost-of-living calculator. They even offer tips on how to increase the resale value of your home, for example, replacing your floors, giving your cabinets a facelift, painting the exterior trim on your house, and other valuable spruce-up suggestions.

No wonder *Fortune,* in 2003 and again in 2004, praised Lowe's, which has been around since 1946, as the "most admired" specialty retailer. It is abundantly evident that Lowe's *cares* about improving not just your home but also your quality of life—"improvement" in the broadest sense. Lowe's manages to impart this caring even though they are a huge company that has 1,050 home improvement stores in 46 states.

Although a busy businesswoman, after attending a how-to clinic or browsing Lowe's Web site, may not buy a tool or product immediately, she's still left with a warm, fuzzy feeling about the company. And, as we now know, women tend to act on their feelings and share them with others.

One last word on Lowe's: the store atmosphere appeals to women. Sales clerks know the merchandise and are always extremely helpful. When I visit Lowe's, I never feel like I'm walking into an all-male atmosphere for the kind of guy who uses power drills on a daily basis. I'm encouraged by them and get the impression that I can actually improve my own home!

Let Consumers Take Your Product for a Test Drive

You've seen women squeeze melons in the supermarket and try on clothing in dressing rooms. Women want to touch, feel and test, or even, when appropriate, *taste* your product. Tasti-Delight, the frozen yogurt chain, offers free samples of their daily flavors, and tasters invariably buy a cone! I had an experience with another smart company a few years ago while I was attending a NAWBO conference in Orlando, Florida. Jaguar was a sponsor, and I got to actually test-drive a Jaguar. Later, I bought one. Before this experience, I thought Jaguar was out of my price range and generally unsuitable. However, first I saw that the company was supportive of women business owners. Then I got to talk with a helpful salesman who encouraged me to get behind the wheel of a Jaguar for a lovely test drive. I realized then that buying a Jaguar was entirely possible and even appropriate for me.

I was as impressed by that salesman, who patiently answered all my questions, as I was by the car itself. I truly felt like I was being educated, not sold. As it happens, I didn't buy the car right away since, at the time, I was leasing an SUV. The minute the lease expired, however, I did purchase a Jaguar, and have not regretted it for a moment. The car gets more mileage than my husband's SUV, seems safer, and is definitely easier to drive. I work hard—why *shouldn't* I enjoy myself and treat myself to a snazzy car if I can afford to?

Jaguar's XJ Series was one of the ten best cars for executive women, according to a list compiled by Edmunds.com, the automotive Web site. The editors at Edmunds.com called the XJ sedan "a huge leap forward in terms of quality, technology and performance," and "a modern classic." The car boasts rich wood trim, soft leather and a new aluminum infrastructure. It's great to feel I'm on the cutting edge! (By the way, in case you are interested, the Mercedes-Benz E-Class and SL-Class, the Lexus RX 330, the Audi A8 and the BMW 6 Series also made the top ten.)

It turns out that my attitude is fairly typical of professional and executive women earning at least $100,000. Many successful women look for style and status when they choose a car. Since luxury cars *are* expensive, we also want value and reliability. No wonder most Mary Kay Directors drive Cadillacs! Sarah Lee Marks, manager of Corporate Fleet Sales for the Integrity Automotive Group, told me that her women executive clients often pick a smaller car that's a luxury status brand, instead of a larger car from a brand with less flair. Her women executive clients seek things like fuel economy, free scheduled maintenance (which means reliability and that upkeep cost will not be an issue), and also good lease terms. Such brand differences can make or break a deal.

Beyond the Test Drive – the Test Bake, or Sip...
At one of their new stores, in Costa Mesa, California, Maytag, the venerable appliance company, built ovens in oak cabinets and demonstrated how to bake chocolate chip cookies, bread and pizza in those beautifully appointed ovens. Maytag stores feature full cooking demonstrations and classes. They and other appliance experts take the time to educate customers about their various products.

Whirlpool, for another example, opened a 12,000 square-foot public showroom and innovation laboratory called an "Insperience Studio," where they allow consumers to test out Whirlpool and KitchenAid appliances. Many wine stores in New York and elsewhere hold free tastings to educate customers about varieties of wines from different regions and countries. If you've ever been to a wine tasting at one of these stores, for example, Astor Wines & Spirits or Vintage New York, which are both in Manhattan, or a wine store called Big Nose Full Body in Brooklyn's Park Slope, you will see those tasters lined up at the check-out counter. Tasters are buyers!

Think tactile. Think touch, test, taste, smell, sip or drive. Make sure your product or service woos at least two of a woman's senses.

Companies That Provide Education: North Fork Bank
What could be more natural for a bank than to offer free seminars on financial topics? I helped one of my clients, North Fork Bank, offer free monthly early morning breakfast seminars at its branches in New York City. Women business owners were invited to attend—and they did! We initiated this program in 2001 by talking to a focus group that consisted of highly-influential women professionals and business owners. Half of them were North Fork customers, half were not...yet. We met in the bank's boardroom. We asked these successful women to share

their feelings about what was good and bad about banks in general, and also what financial issues they might want to learn more about. The women welcomed the opportunity to share their opinions. Be forewarned! Women *do* tend to be honest about their feelings, so be prepared for an honest answer, whether or not it's what you wanted or hoped to hear—and then act on it!

After this particular focus group, we found experts at North Fork who could discuss topics that drew the strongest interest. These included exit strategies for selling a business or passing on a family business, and estate planning. Next we asked North Fork branch managers to invite women business owners to women-only breakfasts at New York restaurants—restaurants with whom North Fork does business, of course. The women-only part was important. Many women feel more comfortable asking questions in an all-female group. Perhaps they think men have all the answers—not because men *do*, but because men often don't ask questions, even if they are completely in the dark. Don't ask me why. Maybe it's the same gene that prevents men from asking for directions when they're lost.

North Fork had already held an all-day financial management program for small business owners, and always attracted a lot more men than women. I convinced them to do it for women only. It turned out to be a win-win event: the women enjoyed it and learned a great deal, and the restaurants enjoyed it because the bank showcased the restaurants for an audience of local business owners *and* picked up the tab. The bank, of course, was happy to be reaching their target audience. We gave the women time to network as well so they were happy on many levels. I always encourage the women who attend these events to socialize and build relationships with each other as well as with the sponsor's staff. The bank was even happier when many of the attendees became their customers, opening checking and savings accounts and using them for mortgages, loans and other North Fork products.

By the way, for educational events that continue over more than one day, it's important for the same staff to attend in order to allow relationships to develop with the attendees. It's hard to develop a relationship if a different staffer shows up the next time you go, someone without a clue as to who you are or what you do. In that case, you have to start over from scratch to get reacquainted. This can makes you feel you're not even dealing with the same company.

Tell Me a Story
Storytelling is a powerful and exciting way to bring your information to life. In your marketing and PR materials, advertising and all other outreach programs, you should ideally describe the benefits in human terms: how your product or service changed a woman's business or life. This is far superior to discussing your products or services in the abstract. Let's say you are an insurance company and sell disability insurance. Tell a true story about a client, for instance, a businesswoman who purchased a policy, then later developed a serious illness and could not work for a year. Relate how the insurance she purchased made all the difference for her. Or perhaps relate an anecdote about a woman who *almost* bought a policy, then did not, with unfortunate results. Stories put a human face on your product or service and make your message real and relatable.

Case Study:
Syms: An Educated Consumer
Syms, the famous off-price designer and name-brand clothing retailer located in New York City, is as well-known for its brilliant trademarked slogan, "An Educated Consumer is Our Best

Customer," as it is for its strategy of dropping prices the longer an item stays unsold in the store. Its president and spokesperson is a woman, Marcy Syms. Why am I not surprised?

The Syms Web site takes education seriously, and uses their online site to educate customers on such subjects as job interview clothing tips for women and men, dressing tips for different industries from banking and law to the creative professions, how to tell if your clothing fits you well, and so forth. These are wonderful ways to engage your customers and show you care about them and their satisfaction and success.

Why Advertising (By Itself) Isn't Enough...
NEWS FLASH: Don't shoot the messenger, but advertising alone does not work if you are seriously trying to reach women in business. Advertising may be a multibillion-dollar industry, but if a company does nothing to establish contact with living, breathing businesswomen, this money will go to waste. Getting involved in live events is critically important, whether this means offering your own live events, or sponsoring or attending events that reach businesswomen, such as our conferences. Your employees, executives and sales reps need to meet the businesswoman customer, build Community with her, create a Relationship, Educate her, Anticipate her needs, build her Trust, Entertain her a bit, and give her excellent Service and Support. Is this beginning to sound familiar? That's right, you do need to put *every* aspect, every step of the C.R.E.A.T.E.S. program into play to capture a customer and insure that she will become and remain loyal to your brand.

Advertisements too often focus around one snappy phrase or TV sound bite. Also, and this is one of my pet peeves, some companies far too often use an attractive woman in a bikini or other sexy outfit to pitch the product, an obvious attempt to subliminally equate sex with whatever they are trying to sell us. Likewise, many print advertisers seem to believe that plunking an attractive "dressed for success" woman into their ad will automatically make the product or service appeal to *women*. Excuse me, but what are they thinking!

First of all, if there's not enough substance to interest (read "educate") a smart businesswoman and show her the benefit, *why* should she want that product? Secondly, do advertisers really think that women are going to be won over to their product or service by featuring a woman wearing a super-sexy outfit or even a business suit? And if that is not the case, if they are directing their ads to men, do they think women are not the ones making the most buying decisions?

As I stated earlier, we women are responsible for 85% (or more) of all purchases.

Another thing for companies to think about is getting their message across effectively, which takes more than a good-looking actor or a clever ploy. I can't tell you how many times I might remember an ad that was funny or had a catchy jingle, but completely missed recognizing what product they were trying to sell, or instantly forgot it. For these reasons, I am continuously struck by how off-base advertisers can be. In a recent TV ad campaign for a major canned tuna manufacturer, the spokesperson was a tall, dark and handsome tattooed guy with a muscular body and a big smile. In this ad, Mr. Muscles sidles up to a woman in a supermarket aisle and asks her what she's looking for. She says, "Hunk tuna, I mean chunk," then swoons. The hunk then crows that he knows what women want and is making sure he gives it to them. He then rides off into the sunset on a motorcycle.

Does this canned tuna manufacturer really believe this kind of promotion is going to sell tuna to women? We're concerned about whether or not a food is healthy—for example, whether there is mercury in the tuna, or whether it's loaded with preservatives. We don't need a good-looking man selling us. There are ways to be clever and funny to get across a message, and this to me is definitely not one of them.

Any intelligent person knows full well that ad space is bought space. The advertiser can brag that its product is the greatest thing since sliced bread, but women don't "buy" this. Women are impressed by advertising that provides us with information and thus helps educate us.

An article in a newspaper or magazine, or a segment on radio or TV, has much better credibility for a company since editorial coverage is third-party endorsement, and usually quotes real people, whether they are experts or "real people."

Thus, public relations is a powerful way to reach people's minds and hearts. Women often cut out articles from magazines or newspapers that tell them about an interesting travel destination, a money or health issue, or whatever attracts their attention. They will sometimes keep these clips for years. I know I do, and I have patronized those featured companies because I liked what was written about them.

Please understand that I am not saying not to advertise. Advertising is an important part of every integrated marketing campaign. However, I am saying that advertising is not—by itself—the best way to reach the new affluent market of women in business.

The Magic of the Personal Touch

Woody Allen was right when he reportedly said that 80% of success is just showing up! Actually showing up and *listening* to what the consumer has to say has more credence than a mere ad. When sales reps speak with a potential customer, they should write down what the businesswoman says, whether it becomes an idea for their company's next seminar, or she tells the rep about a personal hobby, or she even shares the name of her spouse or child. Have the rep put that information on the back of her business card if possible. Hey, aren't *you* always flattered when someone you met once remembers something about *you* the second time you meet them?

Women remain fiercely loyal to a company that takes the time to teach them something relevant to their lives, especially when they consistently work with the same company representative, one who remembers the things they said and the issues they discussed. This personal attention communicates that the company is listening, and is about giving, not taking. This point is also crucial in terms of building the "T is for Trust" in the C.R.E.A.T.E.S. program, which we'll discuss in a later chapter.

Women Are Not All the Same

The biggest challenge here is that most companies tend to look at women as one market, period. They think we are all the same. They don't separate us into stay-at-home moms, women with home-based businesses, women owners of larger businesses, women professionals such as lawyers, doctors, accountants and consultants, or corporate executive women. While we do all have things in common, each group is also distinct. And within each group, we need each other in order to create a sense of community.

Lumping all women together is as misguided as putting all

men, or all African-Americans, or any other special interest or ethnic group into one homogenous grouping or category. Advertisers would not (or should not) pitch the same products and price points to a male high school dropout as they would to a male CEO Ivy League graduate who travels by private jet. Why do this to women? To maximize marketing opportunities, it is not smart to ignore differences in the women's market. While you can address women as a gender for certain products (i.e. tampons or casual clothing), it is a wiser approach to recognize and allow for the real differences in women's lives, in their work-related interests, and in their hobbies, some of which might even make them more akin to men with similar careers and education than they are to other women.

IKEA: Recognizing and Honoring Our Different Needs

IKEA is an example of marketing to women the right way. Currently they are launching a small business initiative with a focus on female business owners. The budget-priced Swedish furniture chain recognizes that women primarily initiate and influence the family buying decisions for the home, and that they are the ones who get the family to IKEA. A big "aha" moment came to the CEO of IKEA, North America, Pernille Spiers-Lopez, on the day in 2004 that she spent at a Women's Leadership Exchange conference in Long Beach, California. We had invited Pernille to be our closing keynote speaker because we appreciated the brilliant changes she made in the company that enabled her employees to strike a good work/life balance. Before that day, Pernille was not aware of the growth and purchasing power of women business owners. Hearing the other speeches, meeting and talking with many successful women leading businesses in multiple industries, she had a clarity and breakthrough awareness that allowed her to recognize an exciting new opportunity for IKEA.

Thanks to her visionary leadership, IKEA now has a terrific "small business" area. The furniture that used to be thought of as only for the home office is now arranged to serve customers who have offices or businesses outside the home. I know that I myself once furnished my entire outside office with IKEA furniture, including desks, storage units, credenzas, chairs, and a table from the dining room section that I used as a conference room table. It was all so reasonably priced and good-looking that my clients and visitors never knew it was IKEA. By the way, it's no surprise that most often the person who knows best how to reach women is...a woman.

Pernille's realization at her first WLE conference experience led to her creation of a strategy for IKEA to market to women business owners and to women who help their husbands create the interior design, set-up, arrangement or selection of what they need for *their* businesses. In less than one year, IKEA set up a small business area in many of its stores, with a full roll-out planned in all its North American stores in the next two years. This area features multiple sample room settings designed for a variety of different businesses, from offices, to hair salons, to spas, cafes and wine stores. You name it and IKEA has the suitable furniture, storage, organization pieces and accessories.

Interestingly, IKEA always has had this furniture and accessories line, but they were never before focused on the women business owner—and these items, spread out all across the various departments of the stores, was far less appealing, and educational, than seeing what kinds of rooms were possible all in one place. (One aspect of education, after all, is learning how to put disparate parts together!) Additionally, IKEA is launching an internal marketing plan to women-owned businesses using the C.R.E.A.T.E.S strategy. And, of course, (forgive me for mentioning it, but we are thrilled) they have become a national partner of Women's Leadership Exchange to help move that strategy forward with velocity.

Case Study:
White Dog Cafe: Food for Thought
The White Dog Cafe is a one-of-a-kind Philadelphia restaurant where founder and CEO Judy Wicks has set up a program that educates customers about the kinds of social policy issues that she believes *should* be important to them. Under her leadership, the restaurant hosts Monday night lectures, a Sunday night film series and offers storytelling on topics that include health care, globalization, war, abortion rights, prison reform and how service dogs help the disabled. The company also organizes tours for customers and employees to Cuba, Mexico, Nicaragua, Vietnam, Israel, The Netherlands, Lithuania, Palestine and other parts of the world in a further attempt to foster understanding of the effects of U.S. policy.

Since White Dog's four-pronged mission is "serving customers, community, employees and the natural environment," the company also sponsors community service projects such as planting trees and sending books to prisoners. White Dog organizes tours of solar-powered and sustainable houses, and, through its sister restaurant program, arranges dinner parties in minority-owned sister restaurants in Philadelphia and nearby Camden, NJ. They pay entry-level employees a living wage and mentor inner-city high school students interested in the restaurant business. Their adjacent gift shop, The Black Cat, features local crafts as well as those made by workers' cooperatives from Africa to Latin America.

Twenty percent of the cafe's profits go to the White Dog Foundation, which supports over 100 family farms, helps 200 members of the Sustainable Business Network of Greater

Philadelphia, and awards grants, equity investment and free consulting services to local firms whose business plans show their bottom lines are measured by "people, planet and profit." One hundred percent of the restaurant and gift shop's electricity is wind-powered.

All this shows that Judy Wicks puts her progressive ideas into practice. Not surprisingly, the White Dog Cafe has attracted a devoted and loyal following that patronizes the restaurant, participates in its projects regularly, and donates to its Foundation. Wicks started the restaurant as a takeout muffin shop in her home in 1983. She has since won many honors and awards, including the Business Enterprise Trust award founded by Norman Lear of "All in the Family" fame for creative leadership in combining sound business management with social vision. She was also awarded *Business Ethics Magazine*'s first "Living Economy Award." She is on *Inc. Magazine*'s list of "25 favorite entrepreneurs in the U.S." and *American Benefactor*'s "America's 25 Most Generous Companies." A former chairman of the Social Venture Network, now an emeritus advisory board member and national cochair and cofounder of the Business Alliance for Local Living Economies, this is an amazing woman business owner who truly believes in "walking the walk." Judy Wicks is a superb illustration of the "E" for Education in our C.R.E.A.T.E.S. strategy. No wonder Gloria Steinem, keynote speaker at WLE's 2004 conference in New York, praised her so highly.

Chapter 5

A is for Anticipate:
Know What Your Customers Will Need
Before They Ask For It

> *"I think the one lesson I have learned is that there
> is no substitute for paying attention."*
> ~Diane Sawyer (1945-) journalist

Businesswomen are loyal to companies that take them seriously by listening to what they have to say, and then anticipating their needs.

One thing that woman business owners want most is a flow of new business leads. Think about how you can help her get new leads. If she's a corporate executive, can you find a way to help her advance more quickly through the ranks within her corporate structure? How can you help the women business owner attract new business? Another commodity none of us women business owners ever have enough of is *time!* Can you save us time or make things more convenient for us? These needs may not immediately seem to be directly related to the sales cycle, but, believe me, they are an important part of the pre-approach and post-service phase.

Think about what businesswomen's lives are like, what our mindset is, and what we need to make our lives easier and less complicated. Can you help us compulsive multitasking women handle all our projects more easily? If you can, we'll love you for it and buy from you.

When you're marketing to a woman, be sensitive to the realities of her busy schedule. Rather than offering only one product, offer her choices so she won't feel compelled to do additional research with competitive vendors because you've given her options.

A Native American proverb tells us to not to judge a man until you have walked a mile in his moccasins. Relating that to today's businesswoman, you don't have to walk a mile in our moccasins (or our high heels). Just ask us what our lives are like. We'll be happy to tell you!

Case Study:
Wyndham Hotels: Making a Home Away From Home More like Home
When you travel on business these days, have you ever noticed that the beds seem to be more comfortable, the bathrooms bigger and better-appointed, and that the work area seems to be more workable? Also, have you noticed that there's a better selection of snacks in the minibar? Well, if so, you should also know that you have women business travelers to thank, women who voiced their opinions on their likes and dislikes about hotels. They created a ripple effect in the hospitality industry, and then men decided they *also* liked these improvements, which clinched the deal.

The hotel industry is still male-dominated...well, at least for now! Executives in that arena used to totally ignore the fact that women travel a good deal, let alone travel for business! As a result, nobody had tapped the women's business travel market—that is, nobody until Wyndham Hotels and Resorts. Wyndham was the first in the industry to break from the pack. They didn't have to read women's minds—they actually *asked* women what they wanted from a hotel. When they had the answers, to their eternal credit (and their enhanced bottom line), they acted on it.

Wyndham began surveying both women and men business travelers in 1995, with the help of New York University. They actually formed a Women's Advisory Council, which consisted of women who travel frequently on business, to discuss what was wrong about hotels and how to improve them. Armed with that feedback, and under the able leadership of Cary Jehl Broussard, a pioneer in marketing to women business travelers, Wyndham created their breakthrough "Women on Their Way" program. I am happy to report that this program, which was specifically designed to appeal to women business travelers, has grossed in excess of $300 million in revenues from women business owners to date. This once again proves my contention that marketing to women in business not only earns you their loyalty, but it is also *extremely* profitable!

Cary is now a dear friend of mine, and I have been a member of this Advisory Council for the past three years.

Today beds in Wyndham hotels feature pillow-top mattresses for cozier sleeping, and bathrooms feature upgraded amenities from the Golden Door Spa, a luxury spa chain that Wyndham now owns. And wait until you hear this: domestic long-distance phone calls and in-room high-speed Internet access are provided to frequent travelers for *free* when you sign up for the "Wyndham by Request" program (at no charge). Healthier foods like salads and light fare are offered in all its restaurants. If you order room service, you get a call about ten minutes before delivery to tell you that your food and drinks are on the way so that you don't have to wonder who's knocking on your hotel door and can be dressed and ready when the knock comes—instead of in the shower. Also, desk chairs are ergonomically designed to make deskwork more comfortable.

The smart program they initiated, "Wyndham by Request," allows guests to customize their hotel experience with pre-arranged choices of free snacks, including fresh fruit, cheese and crackers or trail mix. You can also pre-choose your bed size (king or doubles) and your room location. All this evolved from Wyndham's women's program, which has been an enormous success. Wyndham was also one of the first hotel chains to have coffeepots in the room—a dandy idea if you want a quick cup to wake you when you first get up, or don't have time for breakfast. Altogether, its guest rooms have become more appealing and functional for business travelers of both genders, more like the "home away from home" these rooms are supposed to be. They even offer women business travelers an easy-to-follow, entertaining exercise DVD showing them how they can work out in their hotel room, using room furniture as props—no sneakers needed!

No wonder Wyndham is now the official hotel for many women's groups, including Women's Leadership Exchange. We also hold our women's business spa retreats at the Wyndham El Conquistador Hotel and Golden Door Spa in Puerto Rico and the Wyndham Boulders Resort and Golden Door Spa in Arizona. Business and Professional Women USA also books their events at Wyndham hotels. The chain is a sponsor of our WLE conferences. A Wyndham hotel weekend is a raffle prize, and each of our distinguished COMPASS award winners receives a gift from Wyndham—free attendance at one of our business spa retreats.

Attention, Retailers:
Direct Selling to Women Isn't Just Tupperware
Many traditional retailers, including clothing retailers, fail to take advantage of opportunities to reach out to the powerful women in business market. They don't address the critical need women business owners, executives and professionals have to dress and accessorize well, and in general, look well-groomed, most if not all the time. To me, this means that these business owners or executives may not understand how much most of us want to dress well but simply don't have the time to wander through department stores or wait on long lines to try on clothing. That's why we would deeply appreciate department store shopping consultants who could meet us personally and access our needs, or, ideally, help us find what we want and, perhaps, bring choices directly to us in our homes or our offices.

Companies that sell directly to women by appointment through showroom, home and office sales are a godsend to time-pressed businesswomen who need sophisticated clothing and accessories. According to the Direct Selling Association, direct selling of products one-on-one is a $30 billion business! The women's high-end clothing niche, which includes direct-sellers like The Carlisle Collection, founded in 1980, The Worth Collection Ltd., founded in 1991, and Nina McLemore LLC, founded in 2003, accounts for about $350 million a year of this $30 billion, estimates Caroline Davis, CEO of The Worth Collection. This is what I call an underutilized opportunity.

Case Study:
Nina McLemore: Style, as well as Substance, for the Businesswoman
Nina McLemore was the managing partner of Regency Capital, a venture capital firm for small to mid-sized businesses. She had also served as president of Liz Claiborne Accessories. From

her own experience and that of other busy, successful women like herself, Nina recognized that many professional and executive women were having a tough time finding smart, stylish clothing suitable for meetings, business travel and special occasions. In the time-honored tradition of "If you can't find what you want, do it yourself," Nina, who has also served as chairman of the board of the Center for Women's Business Research, designed her own clothing line for this underserved, high-income niche. Today her clothing line is made up of luxurious fabrics, simple, clean lines, flattering colors, and an easy-to-mix-and-match selection of separates that "play well together" and also travel well.

Acknowledging what businesswomen's lives are like, Nina's independent sales reps show her collection four times a year, continue to sell regularly throughout the year to the customer base they developed, and constantly work at expanding it. The Nina McLemore collection fits every shape and size, and is not just for the anorexic-looking models you see in most fashion ads. The line includes fabulous jackets with detailing that can change the look of an outfit. She does a great job designing the kind of wardrobe a businesswoman needs for travel and leisure. Her customers can easily order the three, four or more new suits a year they need from her line. I know this because I recently bought a great outfit from her collection. This dress ensemble doesn't wrinkle, and after six hours of wear, looks like I just put it on. I've also bought some striking suits and tunics in black and white. Her prices range from $65-$900, which isn't ultra-expensive. She doesn't accessorize, but does display accessories from other designers at her showroom presentations. These showroom presentations are also networking events where businesswomen chat with each other over wine and snacks. Besides giving these women what they want and need, the foundation of her great success is that she's thought it all through completely!

Tech Products That Make Our Lives Easier

Technology is wonderful...and frustrating. So many technical manuals and even ads seem to be written in what I call "geek-speak." They do not realize it, but their materials are definitely male-oriented, with too many numbers and specifications. Like the male-oriented selling style I discussed earlier, there is no emphasis on aesthetics or convenience. However, the good news is that some companies are trying.

I have a BlackBerry and I love it. It's really fantastic for women. I can type messages on the plane, sit by the pool or in a golf cart, and read my e-mail, or send messages to someone sitting in the same meeting. I used to read e-mail on my laptop in my hotel room from 11 p.m. to 1 a.m. Now, while I still bring my laptop for writing and other more extensive computer needs, I can grab my Blackberry and respond to e-mails throughout the day. Then, when I return to my hotel room, I can spend less time on e-mails and focus more on preparing my presentations for the next day on my IBM ThinkPad.

With all the traveling that businesswomen do, it can get lonesome for us on the road. It's nice to be reminded of those near and dear. Some of us put family photos in our hotel room to make it feel more like home. But there *is* another alterative. Apple's iPod, the digital music player that at first started for kids, is now popular with baby boomers, especially women who travel for business. As well as storing your favorite music on the iPod, you can also store your favorite photos. As you travel around the world, you can have your "family photo album" with you at all times, and can, if you like, share them with people without carrying 30 photos in your wallet, or even photos in frames! This makes travel less lonely, and you know how we women enjoy sharing pictures!

Apple iMacs are also intelligently designed for women. They come in attractive colors such as peach and blue and other colors that can actually blend in with the color scheme of your room or office. Most desktop computers look like ugly pieces of equipment that stick out like a sore thumb in a living room or bedroom, despite the fact that many women today have home offices or work from home at night. This is another ingenious example of Anticipation—intuiting that women might like an attractive, stylish, computer.

Hewlett Packard also has the right idea! Their new printers make downloading photos off your digital camera so easy to do. You simply insert a memory card, without the need to download all the photos into your computer first. HP *anticipated* the technical frustration women have, and our lack of time, and came up with a way to make this process easier for us. I can tell you that their devices are simple and easy to use. And believe me, I'm no techie!

Case Study:
Fresh Direct: Gourmet Food Brought to Your Doorstep
Most stores will deliver, but I sometimes wonder what the point is of grocery delivery if you still have to make the trek to the supermarket, shop, and then wait on line to check out? Well, Fresh Direct allows you to order fresh meat, seafood, cheese, produce, wine, herbs and spices from its Web site (www.freshdirect.com) with next-day delivery in many New York City neighborhoods. Its prepared foods department allows customers to choose gourmet entrees such as coriander and peppercorn-crusted tuna, Cajun-blackened salmon, steamed lobster, and a variety of soups and appetizers.

Fresh Direct tries to live up to its slogan "Our food is fresh. Our customers are spoiled." They deliver up until 11:30 p.m. on weekdays, earlier on weekends. They cater parties, and have a quick-shopping feature online that makes it easy to order and reorder, once you've composed your grocery list. There's a 100% guarantee of replacement or refund if a customer isn't happy. Even better, and this may sound difficult to believe, prices tend to be even lower than supermarkets because the company deals directly with farms, fisheries and dairies, thus cutting out the middleman.

Fresh Direct is a terrific example of A for Anticipation. We all have to eat every day, so Fresh Direct anticipated women's need for delivery without having to actually go to the store, our need for extended delivery hours, our desire for a choice of fresh quality products, our occasional desire for catered meals, from soup to nuts, and our appreciation of easy reordering. The company founders thought through what harried or even *exhausted* business people need and then set out to satisfy these needs. Their food deliveries come directly to the customer in the same way that The Carlisle Collection, The Worth Collection and other direct-selling women's clothing companies do. In addition, what Fresh Direct does is also R for Relationship, since the easy reorder feature encourages repeat customers, and E for Entertainment, thanks to their gourmet offerings and event catering.

Now all they have to do to make *me* happy is come out to Westchester, NY where I live!

Less Time, Fewer Frills Spells Gym Success
One of the fastest-growing franchised businesses around is Curves for Women, a national chain of gyms, which anticipated women's needs for a quick (30-minute), yet intense fitness workout in a for-women-only gym, with no mirrors. This is ingenious on several levels. Many women don't want to "dress up" in designer spandex to go to coed health clubs, which some-

times have a singles-type atmosphere. Also, if you are not in the best of shape, you do not want to be constantly reminded of it in the mirror—it's sometimes difficult enough to have to look at the fit woman next to you! And since we don't want to spend too much time at the health club, a half-hour is perfect, and maybe we can even fit it in more than once a week. Bravo, Curves!

Anticipating Changing Space Needs

Companies need office space, but their space needs often change over time. It's difficult to predict how much you'll need even two years from now, let alone five or more. It's also a hassle committing to a long-term lease, buying furnishings, and renovating whenever your company expands or contracts. This need for flexibility is common to solo entrepreneurs, to start-ups, to small to mid-sized companies, and even to divisions of much larger companies. This need is brilliantly addressed by HQ, a member of the Regus Group. As the largest network of furnished office space, HQ offers office space, shared conference and meeting rooms, and shared office equipment, including photocopiers, fax machines, and even support staff, including receptionists and administrative assistants. HQ has more than 750 locations in 60 countries, including the U.S., Europe and the Far East.

You can rent office space from HQ on a regular basis, rent their communal conference meeting room for one-time use, or have a "virtual office" at their address where your phone can be answered and your mail received at a good address in a professional business district. Among the advantages, if you have a home-based business, your business mail isn't sent to a home address.

WLE headquarters is located in an HQ Global Workplace suite of shared offices on New York's Wall Street. Users of HQ in one city can rent its space in another city when traveling, which is a great convenience. Since we're in HQ space, when I traveled to Chicago for a board meeting, I was able to use HQ space there for a videoconference with people who were located in different parts of the country. This is also a terrific A for Anticipation since HQ is meeting the need that many entrepreneurs and professionals have for flexible space and convenience for their growing companies.

Small Stores Can Anticipate Too

Don't think you have to be a big chain to appeal to business-women. Sometimes a small local store anticipates what we need before we ask for it. Buttermilk Blue, a little gift store in Irvington, NY near where I live, does beautiful gift-wrapping. This service acknowledges that my life is so busy I have no time to do it myself, or even shop for the ribbon and paper. Like every businesswoman I know, I am happy to pay extra for helpful services like this.

In another personal example, after our family moved into a new townhouse community in Westchester a few years back, a man hung a flyer on our doorknob promoting his window treatment business. He was an exclusive sales rep for Hunter Douglas. We called him and he came to see us with his sample books. We spent a couple of thousand dollars with him for lovely window treatments without needing to shop around for what we wanted. Again, this salesman anticipated that a bunch of new residents would want to cover their windows with something and came directly to these potential customers. An entrepreneur like this gets an "A" for anticipating my needs, and will get my business, and repeat business, every time!

Chapter 6

T is for Trust
Proving Your Integrity and Commitment to Your Customers' Success

"The best prospect is the client who has already dealt with you. The second best is the one referred to by a client who has dealt with you previously. The third best is the one referred to you by another trusted professional or friend."

~Marilyn Jennings (1944-)
author of *Championship Selling* and other books

When I say that women in business buy from companies they trust, I mean companies committed to good business practices, with sales representatives and executives who keep their word.

Trust is a fragile thing, easily broken, and at the same time one of the most important factors we businesswomen take into consideration when we choose companies with whom we want to do business. We ask ourselves, what have we *heard* about you? Are other women doing business with you? If so, what was their experience? Do your advertising and support materials communicate that you understand a businesswoman's needs? Or are you, like so many other companies, mistakenly lumping all your potential customers into the same category? In addition to these questions you also need to ask yourself if your representatives treat customers with respect and answer their questions without making them feel foolish or embarrassed. And how are women portrayed in your marketing materials?

Women's trust is not freely given; it definitely needs to be earned. To build trust, your company needs to show integrity on every level with products and services we can count on. For one thing, please don't make promises you can't keep. And, if your product breaks or doesn't work, let us return it with a 100% money-back guarantee, no questions asked, no "Tough, you bought it, it's your problem" type hassles. Ask any woman how she feels about being cheated (or cheated *on*)—whether it's by a company or a husband—and you'll get an earful.

If your company has already walked up the first four steps of the C.R.E.A.T.E.S. program and understands the need to create Community with us, build a Relationship with us, Educate us, and Anticipate our needs, you're on solid footing to begin to understand how to build Trust. Once trust has been established, it's up to your company representatives to show that they can continue to be trusted. If we trust the person who represents a company, we tend to trust the brand. Conversely, if that person does not have complete integrity, it can work in reverse. We are all only as strong as our weakest link.

Ask appropriate questions, and then listen carefully to our answers so that you understand our businesses and our lives. Keep your promises, stay sensitive to our needs, follow through, and treat us with respect. All this contributes to keeping trust alive between you and your customers.

Once you've proven yourself and earned a woman's trust, you

often have a customer for life, and, since we're terrific at refer-rals, you will most assuredly also get many more customers from among that woman's friends and colleagues.

The Gender Gap, Trustwise

I once listened to an interview with Tony DeCicco, coach of the Women's World Cup Soccer team, which had won an Olympic Gold Medal. DeCicco was asked about the differences between coaching men and women. He said, "You can successfully coach men by being in their face and being direct. That's how you gain their respect. But with women, the first thing you must do is treat them with respect and gain their trust. After trust is in place, *then* you can coach them."

Taking a cue from DeCicco, marketers must ask themselves, "What can I do to gain my women customers' trust? How are my sales associates trained to communicate with the female customer?" Let's look at some companies who inspire trust.

Lack of Money: The Root of All Evil for Women Business Owners

Ask any woman business owner what her #1 problem is, and chances are she'll tell you it's getting enough money to fund her business. While woman-owned firms are growing bigger at a faster rate than all other firms, according to reports from the Center for Women's Business Research, they generally start smaller than men's firms. Many such firms also *stay* small because they find it difficult to expand by hiring more staff or buying more equipment. The main reason is that they are undercapitalized. Others suffer cash flow problems due to slow payment on the part of their clients. As a result, women-owned firms may need to borrow significant sums for start-up or working capital, and traditional lenders, unfortunately, are often not interested in making these kinds of loans to women business owners.

Women also tend to lack the traditional collateral men have, and at the same time the conventional credit-scoring system doesn't always fit the realities of women's lives or the types of businesses they are in. Of course, a few decades ago, it was even difficult for a single or married woman to get credit in her own name, so progress *has* been made, but not nearly enough!

Count AMEX In to Help Women Business Owners

Here's how the American Express Foundation and OPEN from American Express demonstrate their solid commitment to women-owned businesses and the challenges they face. In 1999 the company became the first six-figure supporter for the start-up of Count Me In For Women's Economic Independence (www.count-me-in.org).This wonderful nonprofit organization gives much-needed micro loans of $500-$10,000 to businesses owned by women.

Count Me In's CEO, Nell Merlino, the force behind "Take Our Daughters to Work Day" which she launched for the Ms. Foundation, recalls how her agency's relationship with AMEX took off. Initially, Rich Tambor, a Senior Vice President at American Express, helped Count Me In set up a meeting with Fair Isaac, the company that makes credit-scoring software. That meeting led Count Me In to create its own woman-friendly credit-scoring system, which was unveiled at a historic meeting at AMEX offices in 1999, attended by representatives from Fair Isaac, along with Fleet Bank, Lending Tree.com and Acción International.

Once American Express demonstrated its faith in Count Me In's mission by extending them a $100,000 grant, other companies followed suit and offered financial support, particularly British Petroleum (now BP), whose $250,000 contribution was based on the support of Mary Beth Salerno, president of the American

Express Foundation.

Since then, hundreds of women-owned firms have used loans from Count Me In to grow their businesses. One is the Dancing Diablo Studio, an animation production company in Brooklyn, NY. Beatriz Ramos, the founder and owner, initially borrowed $3,500 from Count Me In. Less than a year later, Ramos repaid the loan, and then borrowed another $10,000. She later received a third loan for $40,000. Today her clients include Sesame Street Workshop, Kraft Foods and MTV.

Another success story where a modest direct loan made all the difference is Ethnic Edibles, a Bronx, NY cookie-maker. Owner Heather McCartney borrowed $5,000 for packaging and marketing her cookies, which use molds of traditional African, Puerto Rican and Cuban shapes and symbols. Heather has expanded her product line, and now offers catering and takes orders on her Web site. The company has received lots of local and national publicity that you can view on the Web site (www.ethnicedibles.com).

Trust Begets Trust
Thinking about how the right loan at the right time can make all the difference causes me to flash back to a time years ago when I needed a $150,000 loan in order to hire more employees, buy more equipment and double the size of my firm, Communications/Marketing Action, which then had eleven employees. Frankly, bank after bank turned me down, and I was getting mighty discouraged. Nevertheless, I persevered, and fortunately landed a loan from Flushing Savings Bank, thanks to a wonderful banker named Janet Page, who listened carefully and was sincerely interested in my expansion plans.

Over the years, Janet and I kept in touch. She moved to Fleet

Bank, which is now Bank of America. When I served as president of the New York chapter of the National Association of Women Business Owners (NAWBO-NYC), I asked Janet to convince her new employer, Fleet Bank, to become a sponsor of this organization, and she did! Later Janet, who is highly respected by women business owners, was nominated for the Small Business Administration's Women's Business Advocate of the Year award. I was one of those who wrote her a glowing reference letter, and I am pleased to report that she won the award! I have also sent countless women business owners to Janet for loans.

The moral of this story is that Janet, the banker, representing her company, used her intelligence and intuition, trusted me to repay the bank loan. Because of her faith in me and my future, I trusted her and felt (and still feel) deep appreciation for Janet *and* for Fleet Bank after she gave me that pivotal loan. Janet later also helped the organization of women business owners that I led. I, in turn, was more than pleased to send more business her way and to be able help her win the SBA award. Janet and I had formed a Relationship, one based on Trust. Once that happens, it *creates* many unexpected benefits that flow back and forth between the involved parties.

The Sound of Trust
I'm a fan of the Bose acoustic noise-canceling headphones, which, in addition to their outstanding sound quality, block out ambient noise on flights so I can relax in blissful peace. The headphones are great for anyone who travels on business. I like them so much I also use them at home.
At one point, a little plastic piece broke off my headphones. I brought them to a Bose store and told the salesman I no longer had the receipt. He immediately and unhesitatingly said they shouldn't have broken, apologized for my inconvenience, and

went to the computer to check on my purchase information. He found out I had bought the headphones *18 months ago* (the product was guaranteed for 12 months) and nonetheless kindly gave me a new pair with no hassle. How can you not love a company like that, one with a great product line *and* one you can trust to take care of you if anything goes wrong with their equipment!

Now I tell people not only that Bose makes a high-quality product that cancels noise, but also that they provide reliable and courteous service and an incredible, stress-free return policy. Hear that? That's the sound of trust, coming through loud and clear.

The Look of Trust

I bought a Sony digital camera at Circuit City and while I was on vacation it broke. Sadly, I lost all my pictures. It may have been my fault, but I took it back to the store anyway. The salesperson at Circuit City was like the one at Bose. She apologized for the loss of my photos and immediately gave me a new camera! I was so cheered by this attitude that I decided I could afford the new cell phone I wanted, and bought it from them that very day. The store's policy, and their polite, kind and hassle-free way of backing up their products, proved to me that I can trust them. And I—and most women in business—reward the retailers we trust and tell our friends and associates about them. If nothing else, trust is just good business.

By way of contrast, when I bought a printer at a competitive store, which shall remain nameless, I asked the salesman if it was Macintosh-compatible and was told it was. Well, it was *not!* After struggling with it at home, I finally called the manufacturer's tech people, who admitted it was not compatible with my computer. When I returned the useless printer to the store, they gave me a hard time. For one thing, they asked me the name of my salesman—like I knew! Finally, they did exchange it for another printer, but only amid many grumbles. The damage was done. As I walked out, I gnashed my teeth. I could no longer trust their word or their service, and I have never returned to purchase anything at that store.

Women Remember Snubs

Sometimes, salespeople think it's not worth their while to do business with small companies. Well, guess what they forget: many of these firms are on a growth trajectory and may well become a substantial-sized business! Everyone needs to start somewhere. Our firms may grow, even become famous. Women are sensitive to snubs and aware of how people in business treat them. Just as we remember a kindness, we will remember a snub forever. As we've amply demonstrated, women freely share both good *and bad* experiences. Make no mistake, if we have a bad experience, others *will* hear about it. You definitely want the good buzz from us. One of the easiest ways you can earn our trust is by making sure your salespeople or representatives are courteous and helpful to customers. If you're a retailer, having a smart return policy in place is also key.

I once knew an insurance saleswoman—yes, a woman—who disregarded doing business with a woman-owned fashion firm that she thought was "small potatoes." Five years later, the fashion designer she snubbed, Eileen Fisher, had 32 company-owned retail outlets and boutiques in ten states in the U.S., and more in Canada. Her women's clothing line is now also sold in major department stores, including Saks Fifth Avenue, Bloomingdale's, Neiman Marcus, Nordstrom, Macy's, Dillards, Filene's and Marshall Field's. Needless to say, today that insurance rep would do *anything* to get the account, but guess who can't get her foot in the door?

At CMA, my former PR firm, I instructed my staffers to be extremely nice to everyone, no matter how modest the person's title. Those people we used to deal with at *Vogue* included an editorial assistant named Vera Wang—yes, the world-famous fashion designer. We also dealt with a junior editor at a British fashion magazine by the name of Anna Wintour, now editor-in-chief at *Vogue*.

This is an important lesson. Even if you truly believe a particular woman-owned firm is too small to do business with, maybe you can offer a referral to someone else who can handle her business needs, whatever they are. Or perhaps you can be helpful to her in some other way. Just don't be dismissive and make her feel that she's not worth your time. That snub could well come back to bite you. Also it just isn't kind. There is a quote attributed to the great Greek philosopher Plato that I love: "Be kind, for everyone you meet is fighting a hard battle." I believe that's a good ethic to live by, in business and in life.

Why Establishing Trust is Good Business

A woman-owned business, CBS Coverage, handles much of my company's and my family's personal insurance needs. One of the owners of the company, Sharon Emek, is now much more than a salesperson to me. We initially built a professional relationship through NAWBO. When we met, Sharon took the time to learn about my PR business, and I felt comfortable sharing with her the business challenges I was facing. Sharon generously took the time to listen and to give me excellent advice. Eventually, I needed to purchase new insurance policies. Sharon suggested options other than the products she herself was selling. In terms of our working together, what began with health insurance progressed to casualty insurance for my home, life insurance and event insurance. Sharon is also now a dear, trusted friend!

This is what I would call a no-brainer. It's easier to keep the customers you have—through earning their trust—than be forced to constantly line up new ones because the old ones are gone. Once you win a businesswoman's trust, you can probably also sell other products or services to her. Yet too many salespeople wrongly discount the trust factor. Women in business don't even want to hear a sales pitch from someone who hasn't made an effort to establish trust. And I bet lots of men don't, either!

Chapter 7

E is for Entertainment:
How to Make Working with You Fun as well as Productive

> *"Work is either fun or drudgery. It depends on your attitude. I like fun."*
>
> ~Colleen C. Barrett (1945-)
> president of Southwest Airlines

omen in business appreciate companies that entertain them in some way. Who would not agree with the poet e.e. cummings when he wrote, "The most wasted of all days is one without laughter." And there is an old Yiddish proverb that tells us, "What soap is to the body, laughter is to the soul." Entertain us, make us laugh, help us enjoy our hectic lives a little—or a lot—and you will own us!

"Work hard, play hard" is the mantra most men live by, and doing so makes sense. However, most women in business work hard, and then, instead of relaxing, work even *harder*. They can't seem to fit "play" into their hectic lives. Modern conveniences are part of the problem. Cell phones, e-mail and BlackBerrys are helpful tools, but they also greatly expand the workday. No wonder so many of us are hurtling rapidly towards burnout! Many women do not even take an *annual* vacation, let alone a few shorter "time-outs." This is probably why some of us try to tack on a few days after a business trip in order to unwind, whether alone or with a spouse or partner.

We all need to recharge and renew our tired bodies and spirits from time to time. We need to keep up the enthusiasm, or what the French call *joie de vivre* because that is what inspires us to push through our limits. Thus it is understandable that we businesswomen are eternally grateful to any company that pays attention to our need or desire to enjoy ourselves, especially a company that indulges any or all of our senses, whether smell, touch, taste, sight or sound. Haven't we had enough of advertisers telling us our joy in life should be a new toilet bowl cleaner or vacuum cleaner! Let's look at what we "Wonder Women" really need to get in the right mood or 'tude!

Why WLE Holds a Business Spa Retreat: The New Golf

It's more than "just okay" to take care of yourself and recharge your batteries from time to time—it's an absolute necessity. Businesswomen often need to give themselves permission to do this, which was the rationale behind the development of our Women's Travel Exchange women's business spa retreats, held at the Wyndham El Conquistador Resort in Puerto Rico in winter, and in spring at the Wyndham Boulders in Carefree, Arizona, near Scottsdale. Both hotels feature luxurious Golden Door Spas, and the one in Arizona even provides for meditation in a tepee, where a Native American healer anoints your body with sweet-smelling sage.

What comparable stress-relieving vacations and activities do men partake in? Many play golf, and combine having fun (and getting exercise!) with building business relationships. Well, for women, the spa is the new golf. Sure, some businesswomen play golf, too, but businessmen were the first to make a game of golf a business tool. Combining business learning and networking with an enjoyable vacation is the concept behind WLE's spa retreats.

The focus at our spa retreat is on relationship-building while taking care of ourselves and de-stressing from our busy lives with spa treatments, exercise classes, yoga, stress management and, at the same time, one or two daily workshops designed to help women grow their businesses. High-powered business-women who've attended our retreats include Kay Koplovitz, founder of the cable channel USA Networks and the first female TV network president in U.S. history; Chris Madden, the well-known home lifestyle diva; Gail Evans, bestselling author and former CNN executive; and Gloria Jean, the founder of Gloria Jean's Coffee, a gourmet coffee chain, to name just a few of the incredible women who have joined us.

For some of our attendees, the retreat was their first vacation in years. Others enjoyed it so much they returned to the resort later with their families when business-related workshops were *not* on the agenda.

On one of the four days, under the leadership of Caroline Gundeck, Director of Women's Business Development for Merrill Lynch (a business spa retreat sponsor along with Wyndham), Merrill conducted a workshop on financial planning and had six of their women financial advisors on hand. That enjoyable and informative workshop was not held in a confer-ence room. We were at the Wyndham El Conquistador in Puerto Rico and had taken a ferry as a group to get to an outdoor beach club on a glorious, sun-drenched private island owned by the hotel. As we sat in our bathing suits or shorts and sipped trop-ical drinks, the advisors, each wearing a different-colored straw hat, discussed investments, retirement and estate planning, lines of credit, and so on. Each hat identified a different field of expertise. We were being educated in an unthreatening, actually entertaining and enjoyable way. Since this meeting took place at the end of our spa retreat, and the reps had been there with us the entire time, relationships had already been formed with them in a pleasant atmosphere. In the "real world," after a session like this, reps usually "go in for the kill." Not this time. Talk about the ultimate soft-sell approach! The results have been outstanding for Merrill Lynch with this approach.

By the way, there is only one man allowed at WLE Business Spa Retreats sponsored by Merrill Lynch. That man is Bruce Perkins, Vice President of Supplier Diversity and Business Development. Bruce makes himself useful by advising women, in informal conversations, how they can grow their businesses. He also acts as the "event photographer." He sends great photos (no bathing suit pictures permitted) out to the women via email after the retreat. Between Bruce and Caroline, who has to be one of the most gregarious and focused businesswomen in financial services worldwide, Merrill succeeds in hitting all the steps in C.R.E.A.T.E.S.

Office Depot Holds Its Own Fun-Filled and Educational Event

Office Depot, the office products retailer and another WLE partner, also sponsors its own annual "Success Strategies" conference for women in business at a luxury resort in Florida. The company has been deeply committed to this program for the past five years. Hundreds of women in business from all over the country come to attend their sessions. The program was initiated in 2001 by Lynn Connelly, a former LPGA player, who, along with Office Depot's top management, early on recognized the power of the women's business market. Since the chosen resort also offers a stunning array of spa services, sports and fitness opportunities and relaxing at the beach, Office Depot earns an "E for Entertainment" gold star! Office Depot also has a special section of their Web site dedicated to providing resources for women in business. Additionally, they offer a special "Advantage Card" for women business owners to use to accumulate reward points when they purchase Office Depot supplies and products. Smart move! What woman doesn't like to save money and accumulate points!

Spa Nation

The huge growth of the spa industry is a clear trend that reflects the craving of a great many people, men as well as women, to relax, have fun and, at the same time, end up at least somewhat more toned and attractive. The International Spa Association reports that hotel spas and resort spas have nearly *quadrupled,* increasing from just 473 in 2000 to 1,662 in 2004— and that doesn't include destination spas, where the spa is the main event, not part of a resort.

Destination spas include Canyon Ranch, Miraval and Life In Balance, to name a few. Wyndham's Golden Door resorts are resort spas. SpaFinder.com lists and rates all types of spas. There are also many books you can find at a brick-and-mortar or online bookstore that describe and review both these major types of spas worldwide.

Since the fastest-growing niche in the spa industry is in hotels and resorts, chains are scrambling to either build their own spas, expand the spas they already have (which may consist of only a few humble treatment rooms) or add imaginative new treatments that reflect the region and its culture, such as the yummy (on many levels!) chocolate mud bath at the Hotel Hershey Spa in Pennsylvania, or various popular Native American-inspired treatments available throughout the Southwest.

Since more men now go to spas, smart spas have begun to change their marketing to attract men. In Bermuda, Fairmont Hotels & Resorts Southampton offers a "Gentleman's Barbershop" facial to soothe razor burn, as well as a "Golf Performance Treatment" and an "Up to Par Body Treatment" to massage bodies sore after a day on the golf course. The waiting room of its Willow Stream Spa features a TV tuned to sporting events. And, in another example of catering to men, the Cranwell Golf Club, in its Berkshire Mountains resort in Lenox, MA., promotes its thermal clay treatment as the perfect end to a long day on the links.

Hey, this is not the first time men decided they liked something women thought of first. Nor, I suspect, will it be the last! Remember in our Anticipation chapter, how Wyndham Hotels learned from women business travelers, and how it positively impacted on male travelers as well?

Case Study:
Wegmans: Making Food Shopping Fun
Food shopping is not high on the average person's Top 10 list of fun things to do. So why does Wegmans, the privately-owned supermarket chain, get several thousand letters a year from people *begging* them to open a store in their hometown? (Sadly, they're only located in New York State, New Jersey, Pennsylvania and Virginia.) Why on earth would a *supermarket* inspire such devotion—particularly at a time when some super-markets are losing customers by the droves to mass merchan-disers and discount clubs such as Wal-Mart and Costco? And why are Wegmans' per-square-foot sales figures higher than many of its competitors?

Well, here's the short answer: Wegmans has managed to make

the food-shopping experience *fun*. It's apparently a fun place to work as well: in 2005 *Fortune* ranked Wegmans as #1 in a list of best companies to work for. The chain, which sends its cheese managers to France and California to learn about cheese, believes the two aspects of their business (fun for the customer, fun for employees) are inextricably intertwined.

Free cooking demonstrations at Wegmans include distribution of free recipe cards. All ingredients for those demonstrated meals are in one spot so that the time-pressed businesswoman, if she likes the meal, doesn't have to prowl the aisles to find the necessary ingredients. Clever! The stores are also one-stop shopping meccas. Every Wegmans has a dry cleaner, pharmacy, bookstore, child play area, video rental store, bakery, dining areas and a cheese counter offering over 500 cheeses. Obviously, Wegmans fits into A for Anticipation, too, since they anticipate customers' limited time, our need to multitask, and our desire to accomplish all or at least most of our shopping objectives in one ultra-convenient and truly delightful place.

Case Study:
Whole Foods: Fat Profits from Wholesome Foods

Whole Foods Markets is not only the biggest natural foods retailer in the U.S., it's also the fastest-growing specialty type wholesome foods supermarket in what is a killingly competitive industry. Its 166 stores in the U.S. (they're also in the U.K.) sell everything from meat, fish, vegetables, fruit, cheese, flowers, cat litter and coffee to shampoo, toothpaste, magazines, greeting cards and flowers. These markets have brought chic style to the buying of organic and natural foods. Their beautifully-arranged, well-lit produce displays make it a joy to browse, which by itself is a stand-out in an industry known for grim, hospital-like lighting and zero aesthetics. Offering food as "sensual, succulent succor" is what *Forbes,* in a February 2005 story, called the Whole Foods Markets' secret to success.

Whole Foods Markets also have unbelievable *prepared* foods sections, with a choice of soups, seafood and meat entrees and an extensive sushi bar. The stores host fabulous tastings; for example, just before Valentine's Day they held a well-attended tasting of over 20 chocolate products, from candies to cakes. Strategically-placed placards profile various organic farmer suppliers—a clever use of "R for Relationship." CEO John Mackey, by anticipating his customers needs, strives to make a visit to any other supermarket unnecessary, earning an "A is for Anticipation" gold star from us. Yes, their prices are higher than at other supermarkets, but for many businesswomen that's a no-brainer. After all, time *is* money!

Feeling Clubby on Concierge Floors

Who doesn't like to feel special? That seems to be the modus operandi behind the trend toward special "concierge level" floors in many hotels. This special hotel amenity pampers guests with staffed lounges that serve food at various times throughout the day, often include buffet breakfasts, drinks and hors d'oeuvres at cocktail hour, and in some places lunches and after-dinner desserts and drinks. The concierge lounges and services generally provide fingertip access to news and entertainment in the form of TV sets in a comfortable living room style setting with a choice of current magazines and newspapers, and Internet and Wi-Fi access. Guests whose rooms are on these concierge floors often find the pillows larger, the mattresses thicker, and their turndown service comes with mineral water and chocolates. While there is a surcharge to stay on the concierge floor, the fee is often lowered or even waived for frequent guests. Access is usually by special keycard only.

Who would not leap at the chance to have breakfast or lunch when you want it, especially if you've just arrived, sleepless, from a trans-Atlantic flight? What could be bad about relaxing in a private lounge with a drink, soda or coffee, and be able to chat with a select group of people without venturing into the hotel bar to mingle with the noisy masses? The Hilton, Sheraton, Westin, Ritz-Carlton, InterContinental, Marriott and other luxury hotel chains that offer concierge floors get an "E for Entertainment" as well as an "A for Anticipation" gold star from us for understanding and acting on the fact that many guests, even in deluxe hotels, delight in this kind of clubby, pampered feeling because it addresses not just their needs but also their pleasures. By the way, women also appreciate the luxurious bedding, plump pillows, cozy robes and slippers and bathroom amenities that hotels such as Westin and Sheraton feature in most of their properties. But, please don't forget the full-length mirrors and good bedroom and bathroom lighting. Without this, we can't get dressed with confidence for our business meetings!

Grab a Cup, Pick up a Book, Pull up a Chair

You've got to hand it to the Barnes & Noble and Borders bookstore chains for their breakthrough idea that people may want to leaf through a book before buying it—or maybe even not buy a book on the spot. They also get kudos for turning a bookstore into a welcoming, *entertaining* environment where you can meet your friends or business associates, attend educational talks, have a cup of coffee, or just sit! Borders sometimes holds concerts of new CD releases, and lets you listen to a CD on headphones before you decide if you want to buy it. Barnes & Noble has become famous for its author readings and book-signings. Some of their stores even hold free writing workshops. Both chains offer events calendars so you can see who's speaking at a store near you. They also offer you free shipping for orders of $25 or more if you buy from their Web sites, along with membership cards you can purchase that allow you a 10% discount on every book or magazine purchase. A money-back guar-antee with receipt within a certain time period further ensures customer satisfaction.

These bookstores earn multiple gold stars from us—they have put into play C for Community, R for Relationships, E for Education, A for Anticipates, T for Trust, and E for Entertainment. No wonder their happy customers return to buy again and again. A brilliant use of the essence of our C.R.E.A.T.E.S strategy—and they're not even our clients!

Have a Drink, Admire the Art

I recently became aware of a new phenomenon—which is that many museums nowadays are open on both Friday and Saturday evenings. Their on-site cafés, cafeterias or restau-rants are no longer tucked away in a basement where only those in the know can find them. They also often serve food and beverages in full view of great art. New York's Metropolitan Museum of Art has had great success with its chamber music concerts on weekend nights, serving wine and snacks to blissful music lovers. The Brooklyn Museum of Art's "First Saturday" every month is a big party with free admission to exhibits, live music, dancing, films, talks and children's art activities, all of which draws families in droves from all over New York.

This arts and entertainment trend is not just in the Big Apple. The Dallas Museum of Art, Boston's Museum of Fine Arts, Cleveland and Tampa's Museums of Art, to name a few, have been jumping on the bandwagon to turn art-watching into more of an *entertaining* experience. This means they stay open late on certain nights, offer music that ranges from jazz to classical, and sell food and drinks. In the process, they've lured a broader audience into their facilities, from singles to entire families, depending on the event.

In some museums, the restaurant has become a destination in its own right, adding to the visitor's enjoyment of their overall cultural experience. At the Cafe Sabarsky in New York's Neue Galerie, which is a museum of Austrian and German art, you can nibble on an authentic German Sacher torte and read newspapers in the time-honored leisurely Austrian tradition. *New York Magazine* joked in its January 24, 2005 issue, "One look at the lines for the Viennese-style Cafe Sabarsky, and you may wonder if anyone is upstairs in the galleries."

Women have always been culture lovers, and many have been art patrons, supporting America's most famous museums. Thus it's smart business to host a culture-related event that will appeal to busy businesswomen and enrich their lives. Merrill Lynch, for example, works with non-profits to preserve cultural and educational resources worldwide. They place special emphasis on those museums that enrich local communities where their clients and employees live. This year, the company invited all the women who attended our women's business spa retreat in Puerto Rico to a cocktail reception and private viewing of "Women of the World: A Global Collection of Art." For this exhibit, curator Claudia Demonte had asked women artists from across the globe to answer the question with their art: "What does being a woman mean to you?" The fascinating exhibit, held near the palm-tree-filled court of New York's World Financial Center, was comprised of artworks in many mediums from 177 countries, including Tunisia, the former Soviet Union and Berlin.

Even in Europe, with its tradition of long lunches and siestas, busy professionals and entrepreneurs are succumbing to the workaholic patterns of the U.S. All the more reason for businesses to find ways to combine business and pleasure for their customers. With success-oriented business people devoting longer hours to work, the field is wide open for even more new ideas under E for Entertainment.

Chapter 8

S is for Service & Support:
Backing Up Your Promises with a Smile and
Immediate Assistance

> *"Sow good services; sweet remembrances will grow them."*
>
> ~Madame de Stael (1766-1817)
> French woman of letters

Businesswomen notice the details. Great service and support leads directly to customer loyalty because it lets people know in the best possible way that you care about them and will always treat them with respect and proper consideration.

For women, more so than for men, service makes or breaks the relationship. If they are treated poorly, they won't ever forget it, and your relationship will go down the tubes. On the other hand, making businesswomen feel special with first-class service will result in your earning our business and long-term brand loyalty. First-class service also spins off into first-class referrals. If your company follows the six other steps in our C.R.E.A.T.E.S. strategy and lands a woman business owner's business, capping it off with excellent service and support will ensure that your sales from that woman will multiply many times over.

Excellent service is a pearl beyond price, literally. In fact, service is often more important than price to women in business. You certainly want to pay attention to this crucial seventh letter in C.R.E.A.T.E.S. Take a look at some of the companies that are brilliant at implementing this step:

Case Study: Volvo
Safe, Socially Responsible and Responsive to Women
Volvo cars are renowned for their safety, which is, of course, a major concern for women. Thus it's no surprise that women are an important customer group for Volvo. Studies show that women account for 65% of all Volvo buyers in the U.S. As high as that percentage is, it's actually *more* if you take into account the female influence on men's choice of Volvos. In fact, it is estimated that 60% of cars are bought by women and that women influence the car purchasing decision 90% of the time. Thus almost all car-buying decisions are influenced by women. Europe's percentage of direct female customers for Volvo is also growing steadily.

The Swedish company, although now owned by Ford, has a long tradition of listening to its women customers and meeting their needs. In 2004, a Volvo model debuted that was designed entirely *by* women. This model targeted the most demanding premium customer: the independent professional woman. Dubbed "Your Concept Car" or YCC, its woman-friendly features include more storage space (for laptops, cell phones and other items), automatic door opening, adjustable driver height, good visibility tailored to the driver's build, and a parking assistance button that senses the space between two parallel parked cars.

In 2002, when Camilla Palmertz and other female colleagues presented their ideas to Hans-Olov Olsson, President and CEO of Volvo Car Corporation, he welcomed their input with enthusiasm. "This is a fantastic opportunity for us," Olsson said. "We can concentrate on the fast-growing group of women customers without losing the men, because I'm certain that our male customers will love this concept car." How right he was!

The YCC is a singular, one-of-a-kind car, a Volvo showcase for sharing bright ideas and solutions with the world, but the company has not committed to mass-producing the design. I believe that eventually they will because the most popular solutions to car buyers' needs will be the ones that will stand the best chance of appearing in future models.

Interestingly, Volvo's own customer research found that in the car-buying world's three segments or customer categories—budget, mid-market and premium—the woman buyer in the premium segment is the most demanding of all. We do indeed know what we want!

Back in the 1980s, a women's group was formed at Volvo, and these women were asked to test and assess new models at a very early stage in their development. During the development of the Volvo XC90, a women's focus group was convened in California, and their views helped shape the distinctive features and functions of the company's first SUV. This car won the Total Quality Award™ from the research firm Strategic Vision in the Near Luxury Sport Utility segment for all aspects of ownership experience, driving, owning and buying.

Volvo Cars of North America also deserves praise for the "Volvo for Life Awards," its wonderful awards program that celebrates everyday hometown heroes in America and by so doing helps to encourage and foster social responsibility. Celebrities involved have included Caroline Kennedy, Dr. Sally Ride, Jane Goodall, Paul Newman and Hank Aaron. Winners are judged in three areas: safety, the environment and quality of life, all issues that deeply resonate with women. Past award winners include an advocate for domestic abuse victims, a man who helped Native Americans build housing out of straw bales (a sustainable resource), and a child with cancer who helped fundraise over $1 million for pediatric cancer research through humble efforts such as lemonade sales. Volvo created another awards program for child heroes, named after this girl, who died at age eight— the Alexandra Scott Butterfly Award.

The grand prize winner receives a free Volvo every three years for life. Other winners receive $50,000 donations to their favorite charities. (Nominations for unsung local heroes are accepted online at www.volvoforlifeawards.com.) The awards program is now in its third year.

I'm delighted to report that Volvo helped sponsor our WLE New York conference last year, and offered a $500 discount to any attendee who bought or leased a 2004 or 2005 model by March 31, 2005 (that award-winning XC90 SUV included). That's an additional $500 off, even if the attendee had negotiated any other discounts with the dealer. That is what I call smart marketing!

Roadside Service, Customers Only
Some auto brands, such as Volvo, Jaguar and BMW, offer customers their own brand-specific roadside service, free for the warranty period and renewable for a fee thereafter. Roadside services include repairing flat tires, making emergency gasoline deliveries, and towing to a dealer repair shop so you don't need to call AAA. This can be a blessing, since the latter is only as good—or bad—as the local service vendor. Once my daughter, Sara, was taking our Jaguar to the airport and got a flat tire. A Jaguar roadside assistant arrived in about 15 minutes. If you

are 100 or more miles from home and have not reached your destination, Jaguar, Volvo and BMW also offer reimbursement for lodging and food, along with alternate transportation, such as a loaner, if necessary. This amenity is also free to people who buy certified pre-owned cars from these dealers, again for the warranty period. How handy this is for businesswomen, who often dread a car breakdown in the middle of nowhere!

Apple: Bellying Up to the 'Genius Bar'

At the more than 100 stores Apple Computer owns across the U.S., customers can get free technical support from a live human being for any Apple product at long counters called "Genius Bars." A customer can either book a free appointment online for the same day, or just drop in to see a tech support staffer—called a Genius. If all Geniuses are busy, the customer must wait to be paged. However, if a customer pays an annual fee of $100, an appointment can be booked in advance with a *specific* Genius.

Free tech support is a great service concept. But free tech support with a human being who knows the products intimately, and patiently answers your questions, is brilliant. Too many companies today think they can get away with e-mail customer service, online troubleshooting tips, or endless voicemail systems without a live human. Wrong! That's too cold-blooded and impersonal for most businesswomen. Others expect you to mail the product back and wait for it to be fixed. Okay, what are you supposed to do in the meantime? This isn't enough. The human element is crucial, and nothing replaces the one-to-one encounter. A company that offers only e-mail customer support will never grow a relationship with a woman business owner, or ace any other step in C.R.E.A.T.E.S. for that matter.

Apple Computer has also successfully created a "Community"

around their Macintosh and iPod, has forged a Relationship with their customers, has Educated them, has Anticipated their needs, has created Trust, has Entertained them with attractive-looking, fun-to-use products, and provides stellar Service and Support with its Genius Bars, an ingenious part of its sales strategy.

I use an IBM PC at the office and a ThinkPad when I travel. I also appreciate my G4 Powerbook at home. Thanks, Apple, for achieving S for Service and Support.

Old-Fashioned Service, 21st Century Style

Whole Foods Markets was cited in the E for Entertainment chapter because they turned grocery shopping, normally a dreary chore for most of us, into an enjoyable experience via their gorgeous displays of fresh produce, flowers and fun tastings. While shopping at the health food superstore recently, I received friendly service from three different employees. I asked one man, who was busily restocking shelves, about a protein drink I couldn't find. He suggested another product with a similar taste and nutritional value. Then, looking for popcorn, I asked a second person for help. He stopped restocking and walked me two aisles over right to the popcorn. A third employee said the store didn't carry the frozen VitaMuffins I was looking for, and suggested another brand. Unlike traditional supermarkets, Whole Foods stock employees are trained customer service representatives. They do not view answering customer questions as an interruption but rather consider being helpful an integral part of their jobs.

In the White Plains, NY mall where I shop, Whole Foods also pays for parking for up to two hours as long as you buy $25 or more, and its customers are the only ones allowed to park on the first floor. If you like, an employee will carry your purchases to the parking area and load your car for you. The Whole Foods in Manhattan's Chelsea neighborhood offers free garage parking on the same block for customers who spend at least $75. This, believe me, isn't hard to do, because the company specializes in such a wonderful variety of high-quality products.

All this saves time and frustration for harried businesswomen. Time is money, and, to many of us, little things like this make it okay to pay a little more because of what they add to the "whole" shopping experience.

Back when I was a young girl in York, PA, a supermarket employee would routinely come out and load the groceries into our family's car. Isn't it interesting how some modern companies like Whole Foods, do "innovative" things that used to be considered just old-fashioned service? Unfortunately, that is rare enough nowadays that when a company offers it, women really sit up and take notice.

The Cat's Pajamas Service
Talk to a business traveler, and chances are you'll hear a lost luggage horror story. Either the missing suitcase was recovered too late to be useful, or it remains forever in a Bermuda Triangle of buried baggage. Some of us deliberately don't check our luggage anymore. I once traveled with my husband to the Wyndham El Conquistador Hotel in Puerto Rico, where WLE was planning to (and did!) hold our business spa retreat. We arrived, but our luggage didn't. I explained to the cordial concierge at the hotel that my husband prefers to sleep in pajamas, but that all the resort shops were already closed. What to do? She thought hard and finally suggested lending him a chef's outfit because the pants tend to be really loose and pajama-like. We thought she was crazy.

A few minutes later, an employee knocked at our door and presented us with chef's uniforms in three different sizes: large, very large and absolutely *huge*. She also brought the tall chef's hat! We both had a good laugh—and wondered what the hotel employee thought we were up to! The good news is that my husband found the chef's pants really comfortable and was happy to wear them until our bags showed up. Chalk one up for creative, imaginative service from Wyndham—a hotel chain that not only does a lot to anticipate the needs of women business travelers, as Chapter 5 details, but serves our *husbands'* needs as well.

Worth Their Weight in Platinum

I'm an American Express Business Platinum cardmember. One thing I like about that particular card is their concierge service. You can call and someone will make airline and hotel reservations for you, not to mention reservations at popular restaurants that you might not be able to secure yourself. The concierge can also suggest other restaurants, buy theater tickets, and generally serve as your own personal administrative assistant. It's great if you travel a lot on business and aren't that familiar with restaurants or hotels in other cities. In my opinion, to an overwhelmed woman business owner it's well worth the modest annual fee.

With the Platinum card, you also get these added benefits: a subscription to the upscale travel magazine *Departures,* a newsletter offering tips of interest to business owners, discounts for your business, including office supplies, overnight deliveries and a free companion ticket if you buy a first-class or business-class ticket to Europe. By the way, I took my husband on my recent London business trip, and lots of other businesswomen these days also take their husbands with them on their business trips, so that free companion ticket can really come in handy.

Making Do-It-Yourself Much Easier

IKEA stores are famous for their great, budget-priced furnishings, but you will have to assemble most of the furniture yourself. Fortunately they've added an extra service—you can now hire people to assemble IKEA furniture. Stores have a list of assemblers who are part of a network of independent contractors. For a small fee, they will come to your home or office. I guess IKEA realized that some of their customers—like me!— were all thumbs at this do-it-yourself business. We would try to assemble the furniture ourselves and get frustrated as these wonderfully innovative bargains became a pain in the neck, which can evaporate some of the joy of the low prices. To its credit, IKEA noticed this and responded, making customers like me more confident about buying bigger, more complex pieces. Another company might have said, or implied, "Hey, that's why it's so cheap; it's *your* problem." Not IKEA. Thanks to their great Service and Support attitude, we are no longer forced to struggle through the assembly process by ourselves if we don't want to.

One-Stop Shopping Means Ultra-Convenient Service

PETCO, the chain of stores that sells pet supplies of all sorts, including pet food, toys, leashes, pet beds, carriers, etc., noticed that their pet owner's customers have other pet-related needs. These needs include education about pets, pet health, and even photography (to record that Kodak moment when adorable Poopsie snuggles with his teddy bear). As a result, PETCO offers in-store puppy parenting and dog training classes with a variety of schedules, a walk-in clinic for low-cost vaccinations, testing and other preventive care with a licensed veterinarian (no appointment necessary) and, as I said, pet photography. A machine makes do-it-yourself dog tags. And, if you don't already have a small, furry family member and crave one, or a second or *third* one, you can, on certain days, adopt a dog or cat right in a PETCO store.

Any time a company offers one-stop-shopping, a woman business owner somewhere breathes a sigh of relief, followed by a resounding *thank-you!*

Big Doesn't Have to Mean Impersonal

CDW (Computer Discount Warehouse) is a big company that sells about $5 billion worth of computer equipment and services each year to corporations, schools and government agencies, buying from IBM, Microsoft, Apple, HP, and others. But CDW is also big in customer service—which is unusual for a company that size. Customers praise the one-to-one relationships they have with account managers, who empathize with and respond to their needs, and help them succeed at their jobs or businesses. Founder Michael Krasny's philosophy is that "people do business with people they like." (Where have you heard that before?)

This helpfulness is even more unusual since most selling is done over the telephone. But the sales staff at CDW receives extensive training in customer service, using customer relationship management software that has been designed to capture the likes and dislikes of a customer and other personal nuances. Sales personnel have also been taught to share some bit of personal information with a customer after he or she has shared something personal with them. An amazing winning formula, for sure! They are also amazingly able to answer technical questions in plain language.

Pampering Passengers

Airlines aren't exactly known for good service these days, as pat-downs and shoe removal make flying less pleasant, and "meals" in coach are reduced to a tiny bag of pretzels and a soft drink—or perhaps, if you are lucky, a bag lunch with a cold sandwich, bottle of water and a small bag of chips. At the same time, some airlines have gone out of their way to make business and first-class passengers more comfortable. Virgin Atlantic pampers its "Upper Class" passengers with seats that turn into perfectly-flat beds in cocoons for privacy, sleeper suits and soft pillows on New York-London flights, and even massages and a sit-down bar—which I once had the dubious joy of sleeping right next to! The Virgin Clubhouse in London's Gatwick Airport even offers haircuts, massages and manicures, as well as *lots* of food—not just pretzels—while passengers wait. Cathay Pacific's First Class also boasts fully-flat seats, duvets and sleeper suits, while its First Class lounge at the Hong Kong Airport offers a fine-dining restaurant, a day spa and showers with black polished marble walls.

I'm a member of the American Airlines Admiral's Club—my respite whenever I fly AA. This membership has served my business well since the Club offers private meeting rooms, which saves time compared to driving from the airport into the city for a meeting. Last year, my WLE business partner, Andrea March, and I had an important meeting in Chicago with a very important sponsor, Patti Ross of IBM. We were able to schedule the meeting in the Admiral's Club at O'Hare airport at the end of the day, which was convenient for Patti and for us. Not only was the meeting room attractive and businesslike, it was also stocked with coffee and other beverages and snacks. In all, it was as comfortable as if the meeting had been in our own offices in New York! That meeting was a huge success, thanks to American Airlines' great service. Thank you AA!

I sometimes wonder why airline clubs don't offer waiting passengers the opportunity to network. They can do this by making nametags available for those who are interested, so they can write in their names and companies. I think it would be great, turning hours of waiting into productive time for new business development. If it's really a club, why not act like one and build loyalty? But, of course, networking is the way I view the world. I guess some club members might want to be left alone. Anyway, it's an idea whose time may come at some future point. Don't be surprised if it does!

Service Trumps Price

By the way, high prices don't always equate to a high level of service. Often, there is *no* correlation. Walk into a luxury goods store in a mink, then try it another time in jeans and a T-shirt, and you'll know exactly what I mean. Often salespeople for a high-end brand can be quite snooty and make you feel like you don't deserve the brand. Women customers will remember the service (or lack thereof), not the fact that your company boasts the most beautiful designer jewelry, clothing or leather goods. And we'll tell our friends.

I've noticed that Tiffany & Co. is one luxury retailer whose policy is to treat all potential customers politely and with respect, regardless of how they are dressed, or whether they are buying or clearly just looking. Some of the most casually dressed women may be the owners or CEOs of some of the most successful businesses. And today's lookers are often tomorrow's buyers, especially when you treat us nicely.

Today, in many ways, we do have a brand new world, one filled with enormous and still rapidly growing numbers of active, ambitious, affluent women business owners, executives and professionals. Our numbers and influence have created a new business paradigm, one where the executive and entrepreneurial woman's sensitivities and sensibilities are at the forefront and must be—and increasingly *are*—taken into consideration by any company that wants our business, whether for the short run or the long haul. Now and into the foreseeable future, companies and their brands will live or die by their ability to recognize and accept this reality.

So, now that you know how a savvy company can use our 7-Step C.R.E.A.T.E.S. strategy to capture customers, what are you waiting for?

Afterword
Looking into the Future

Now that you have read this book, you have an understanding of why we call women business owners, women executives and women professionals the "hottest new market." You should now also understand why it is in your best interest to market to them in a different way than you did before, and differently than you may market to other special interest groups or market sectors.

You also now understand why this effort is worth your while, because you will want to attract and make loyal customers of the kind of women who buy for business as well as for their personal and household needs. That is what women entrepreneurs, executives and professionals uniquely do. And that should be what makes them so attractive to you.

As mentioned earlier, men also react positively to the 7-Step C.R.E.A.T.E.S. strategies. In general, however, male entrepreneurs, executives, and professionals are not trying to juggle several balls in the air simultaneously, terrified of dropping any one. Nor do they fully share their female counterpart's appreciation of any efforts companies make to understand and satisfy their needs in order to help make their professional and personal lives easier.

Women's Leadership Exchange was born from a desire to help women grow their businesses and help create more women business leaders overall, and to connect our sponsor companies with this richly rewarding and important market via the C.R.E.A.T.E.S. strategy.

Recently there has been an exciting new development for Women's Leadership Exchange. We are preparing to "go global." Right now we are formulating plans to hold WLE educational and networking conferences for women in business in London and other major cities throughout the world. One thing Andrea and I have learned from our travels to these hubs is that the same principles apply everywhere. The entrepreneurial, executive and professional women we have met on our extensive travels abroad, regardless of where they live or what language they speak, each want and need the same considerations from the companies they do business with as we do here.

While women-owned businesses are the fastest growing segment of the American economy, a sub-stratum of companies owned by minority women is growing even faster. To ensure that the WLE meets the needs of *all* women in business, we recently formed a WLE Multicultural Advisory Council. What we have learned from this group of extraordinary women is that while there are significant differences that must be acknowledged and addressed in order to help up and coming entrepreneurial and executive women grow their business beyond plateaus, women who own or run businesses are far more alike than we are different, and C.R.E.A.T.E.S. works for everyone.

Relationships have always been important and never more so than today. Show a woman that her satisfaction and her company's growth are important to you, and she will give you her business *and* tell all her friends.

It is a brand-new day, and an exciting one. One of the underlying messages of this book is that fun is a big part of all seven C.R.E.A.T.E.S. strategies. When used wisely, these seven steps offer brand new opportunities for your company, and your marketing and sales team, to connect with customers on a superbly more meaningful level.

No matter how intense the competition, if your company creates the right balance with existing and potential customers, you will be the one to capture the hearts and minds of these deeply appreciative businesswomen, who will become your loyal customers and build the best word-of-mouth for you.

If anything is still unclear, or if I can help you create your own multifaceted outreach program to capture this red-hot market, please feel free to contact me.

It's been a pleasure sharing all this with you.

Leslie
www.womensleadershipexchange.com

About Leslie Grossman

Leslie Grossman, president of B2Women (www.b2women.net) and cofounder of Women's Leadership Exchange (www.womensleadershipexchange.com), has been creating business-to-business and business-to-consumer marketing/public relations programs focused on women for more than 20 years. Prior to launching B2Women and Women's Leadership Exchange, Grossman founded and led Communications/Marketing Action, Inc. (CMA), creating public relations and integrated marketing programs for a broad spectrum of industries including new media, financial services, small business, fashion, entertainment, travel and publishing.

During the 14-year history of CMA, Grossman observed companies marketing to businesswomen the same way they marketed to men with disappointing results. As a leader in several professional women's organizations, she noticed the inability of many corporations to translate sponsorships into business. She was concerned that their lack of success would cause them to give up on businesswomen as the powerful market it is. Grossman's experience in marketing to women, integrated with her in-depth study of the businesswoman's market, resulted in her creation of a B2W (business-to-women) strategy, which she began using at CMA. With more and more success with CMA clients, she decided to launch a new company focused on marketing to this elusive group

In 2000, Grossman launched B2Women, established to support the marketing objectives of companies recognizing the power of the fast-growing market of women business owners and business executives. B2Women creates and implements original groundbreaking marketing and public relations initiatives for corporations, women's business organizations, conferences and leading women-owned firms. A track record of successes includes American Express, Platinum Guild International, MetroPartners, SAAB Cars, Northwestern Mutual, BBC and North Fork Bank.

At the time of the launch of B2Women, which coincided with the dot-com crash, Grossman observed mid-stage women-owned firms, like her own, struggling to keep their businesses going. She noted that many lacked the knowledge and appropriate support and connections they needed to thrive and survive in tough economic times. This observation ultimately led to the creation of the Women's Leadership Exchange.

In 2002, Grossman cofounded, with Andrea March, the Women's Leadership Exchange (WLE) as a multimedia communications program with conferences around the country as its centerpiece. Women's Leadership Exchange provides women leading established businesses with the tools, connections and resources they need to grow their businesses exponentially. Based in New York City, WLE also offers leading corporations the opportunity to successfully connect, brand and market to one of the fastest growing business markets today. Now in its fourth year, WLE conferences, which are held in New York City, Dallas, Chicago, Southern California and Atlanta, have attracted more than 8,000 women. Women's Leadership Exchange offers an information-packed Web site, a free business e-newsletter, an online directory, online bookstore, blog and business spa retreats. OPEN from American Express is WLE's presenting sponsor with other prominent corporations as sponsors. WLE is a certified women's business enterprise (WBE).

Grossman has been active for many years in the small business and women's business community including: National Global Chair (2001) and NYC President (1999-2000) of the National

Association of Women Business Owners (NAWBO); National Advisory Council (1996-2000) of the U.S. Small Business Administration (SBA); Counselor, American Women's Economic Development (AWED); and a member of Women Presidents' Organization (WPO). Grossman presently serves on the advisory boards of the Center for Women's Business Research in Washington, DC and Wyndham Women on Their Way. She also served as New York Chair of the Women's Leadership Forum, on the boards of the New York Women's Agenda and Jose Limon Dance Foundation, and Board Secretary of Fashion Group International. In 1999, Grossman was named Entrepreneur of the Year by Fashion Group International and received the President's Leadership Award from NAWBO in 2000. In 2002, Grossman received the Matrix Award from Westchester Women in Communications. In 2005, Grossman and WLE cofounder Andrea March received the Women's Advocacy Award from *Enterprising Woman* Magazine.

Grossman is a frequent speaker on women's leadership, entrepreneurship, branding and marketing to women. She has spoken for four consecutive years at the New York University All-University Entrepreneurship Conference and has traveled as far as Tokyo to address the Tokyo Chamber of Commerce Convention on "Striving Toward a Global Network of Businesswomen for the 21st Century." Other speaking engagements include JP Morgan Chase, The Luxury Marketing Council, Crain's Expo, Commercial Real Estate Women (CREW), the 2002 Annual Meeting and 2003 regional meetings for Northwestern Mutual, Chapman University in Orange County, CA in 2004 and IBM PartnerWorld in 2005.

Grossman received a B.A. in psychology and business from George Washington University, Washington, DC and attended graduate school at New York University. A great believer in continuous growth and training, Grossman is a graduate of Insight Seminars, MAP (Managing Accelerated Productivity) and Landmark Education.

Married to Richard Abrams, Grossman is the mother of two young adults and resides in Dobbs Ferry, NY